Nuance Alley

Life's paths are not always on the map

Karl D. Edwards

Nuance Alley

Life's paths are not always on the map

© 2018 Karl D. Edwards

Cover Design: Nicole Buck
Interior Design: Bernie Sirelson

Dedication

To all those who choose to get back up again...
no matter what knocked you down.

Too Great a Price

I danced a dance
Scripted by others.
I played the game
Laid out for me.
I chose the road
Of least resistance,
Covered my eyes
For the sake of me.

Who betrayed whom may never be clear.
The stories told are fictions from fear.
My dance is now over, and I am to blame;
Murdered for living, exposing our shame.

Cry if you have to.
Scream if you will.
Declare the ship floating
The cruise on due course.
But I from the bottom
Of this faceless ocean
Woke to the dance
And swam for my life.

Myths and illusions cloud with such clarity,
Certain of all we have no way to know.
But when the soul cries for more than right
  polity,
A scandalous evil threatens the show.
Jump through the hoop.
Tickle my fancy.
Your self-esteem
Is now in my hands.
But wait just a minute,
The words are all empty.
It's a beautiful dream
Built on nothing but sand.

These graying temples are weary of dancing.
Sustaining illusions exacts too great a price.
Time to make choices, live freely, act boldly;
Such going named leaving by paralyzed mice.

There's nothing to say when there's so much to
  be.
My confession of death has created new life.
Painful the memory of shattered illusions,
Hope-filled the prospect of authentic lived life.

AWARENESS

Getting comfortable in my own skin.

Every once in a while I catch a glimpse of myself. Usually when I least expect it. In the midst of the busyness that tends to occupy, overwhelm or distract, I will catch myself being me.

More often than not I have no words for describing what I witness. The categories of traits and skills and roles, temperaments and types and jobs don't fit quite fully. It's uncomfortable wearing clothes designed for others. Even if the size fits the style may not.

I am not a category! I chafe and bristle and search for alternatives. Who gets to define these categories, anyway?!

When I am paying attention, I can recognize myself by more than the negative frustration of not fitting into established categories. I can recognize the unique gift I bring to the table. A

gift I bring only if I insist on being
authentically myself.
Listen in as I catch glimpses of myself.

Demanding Invitation

Drawing, inviting,
Irresistibly beckoning
Me forth.
And yet I resist.
Halting, dragging,
Inexplicably holding
Myself back.

Wisdom eludes my grasp
Or I fail to grasp
But with mock determination
The deep work
The good work
The one who is working.

Intention exchanges harsh words
With motivations hiding
Too deep
Not deep enough.

Dueling fears bicker over nuances
While hope lies smoldering in
A forgotten corner.
I stand against
I lean toward
The demanding invitation
To follow.

Confident or Arrogant?

There's not much to distinguish confidence and arrogance. Except that one is based on accurate and sober self-assessment, and one involves no assessment at all, only a positioning comparison over and against others.

I am trying to get more of the one without slipping over into the other.

The voices that accuse of arrogance are imaginary and a mystery to me. But they accuse nonetheless. I don't seem to be able to dismiss them as the irrational nuisances they are.

I need to become more at home with my competencies and wear them more comfortably.

Candor Strikes Again

In this age of perception manipulation and the spinning of reality to achieve narrow agendas, a brush with candor comes as a bracing shock. While initially pitying the naive soul who bleeds voluntarily as the sharks circle, we subsequently catch ourselves remarkably refreshed and secretly envious of their courage and integrity.

By candor, I do not mean emotional exhibitionism. Those people whose pain is so deep that they feel compelled to revisit their shame with anyone who will listen.

In the ordinary course of making decisions, though, responding to problems, choosing directions and interacting with others, our confidence, poise and security can either be a mask we put on or a more natural comfort with ourselves, others and the world. When wearing a mask, the risk of being exposed feels enormous. And so we spin, bifurcate, dance and blame—in short expend vast amounts of energy—in order to keep people from noticing that the powerful visage they have come to trust is but an artificial veneer. When we've made our peace with our imperfections, no mistake, failure or offense can bring us down, because we had nothing to hide in the first place. Very freeing.

It is this freedom that arouses envy and admiration. Far from a naive form of self-betrayal made by those unable to maintain their masks, candor is the deliberate communication choice of the free.

Voices

So many voices. Quite the challenge to discern and distinguish between them. Especially while settling into the integrity of our own. Gone is the adolescent satisfaction of simply being the opposite of those from whom we needed to distinguish ourselves. Down the road always yet is the secure maturity that can listen and learn without ceding self. In the mean time we make our next choices amidst the cacophony of voices we feel expect so much from us. Until, that is, we realize they neither know us nor care about us. No one said growing up would be easy.

Discipline as Training

Discipline does not impose its way upon the will in order to override the will but to train the will. I am not diminished as a person by acceding to an externally governed structure, but am equipped to function better as a person. While there are certainly people and methods which provide forms of discipline in such a way as to diminish and control others, such effects are not inherent characteristics of discipline but dangerous and self-serving manipulations of those involved.

As I begin to recognize areas of life where my will is not serving me well, I would be wise to frame it as an issue of an ill-equipped will rather than a weak will. Rather than get down on myself for continuing to choose poorly, I would be better served to seek out training to teach my will, body, emotions and soul how to pull together.

Such training—while difficult, unnatural and forced initially—would result in a developed capacity, a healthy habit and an alignment between desire and choice.

Who We Really Are

"Love is who we really are." A soul-provoking word from Richard Rohr this morning. Even as I begin to learn that I need to take myself less seriously, the suggestion arrives that while the story includes me, it is not about me.

The route toward a more grounded, secure me is one of freedom. Not the freedom characterized by license or contrasted to constraint, but freedom informed and fueled by love. The best definition one could provide for the responsibility of being free is love.

The inclusion of my very identity in what I have heretofore considered a directive for my will—that of loving, love, lover—gives pause. Something resonates, though I'm not sure I yet understand what or how. Of this much I do know, that I have been given a gift this morning.

Greeting the Morning

A bracing chill floats in the breeze at my back, while the morning sun strives to envelope me in warmth. I greet the morning in all its mystery and potential, and step forward to own the day. An adventure… definitely. A comedy of errors… often. Vintage me… always.

I've already tried not being me. It doesn't work very well. Go figure.

I've tried both qualifying who I am and faking authenticity. To no avail.

I've hidden in the background, pushed my way to the front, painted a smile on, danced till they cheered. You wouldn't believe the crap I've put up with. All in the name of…

Oh geez, I forgot.

Damn.

And then one brisk morning, too exhausted by my own circumlocutions to be other than me, I did a double take in the rear view mirror and decided that this might be someone worth getting to know. A thousand generations of witnesses rose to their feet and applauded and stomped and roared in enthusiastic tribute.

I love the morning.

Real Connections

Connections find their richness in their simplicity. Being nothing more and nothing less than ourselves. People at peace with others being nothing more and nothing less than themselves.

Then people go and change. Enhancing or diminishing their own capacities to experience life. Being ourselves and accepting others then involves supporting or resisting these changes. (Hopefully supporting life enhancing change and resisting life diminishing change.)

Conceptually pure orthodoxies sneak in and capture our attention, with the result that we filter out the people in our lives. We can no longer see each other as we are. We see each other only in terms of what we are not. Connections lose their simplicity and ultimately their richness. In the upholding of the ideal connection, we lose the only connections we have access to, the messy, real ones.

Facing Facts

Facing facts is easier to recommend than do. When the facts do not reflect well on us, we have varying capacities to acknowledge it. In theory, such difficult facts are valuable experiential data from which to learn, change, and benefit. In actuality, though, we keep running up against our fragile egos, unconscious fears, and limited self-understandings, and find ourselves ignoring, overlooking and just plain not able to see certain facts that seem obvious to others. Such is the case with positive facts that collide with a negative self-understanding also.

The issue becomes one of creating safe spaces within which to consider challenging information about ourselves without having to risk a devastating verdict. Of finding safe relationships wherein we can explore without being judged, categorized, or dismissed. Of learning to see facts as helpful clues to a better self instead of damning evidence of an inadequate self.

Fully Present

Getting concrete and specific requires commitment because outcomes can be measured. Much simpler to leave things vague and general. No risk of failure.

Simpler, maybe, but what about getting anywhere? Making progress? Making a difference? What's the deal with avoiding achievement and accountability? As demotivating as I find accountability to others, I accept full accountability to myself and the responsible stewardship of my life. I am stepping up to the plate. I am putting my cards on the table. I rise to meet this next moment. Even as I refuse to bow to all other people, I honor myself and the mandate that inspires me. I know what to do. It's time to do it. It's time to do it all of the time instead of some of the time. Something has changed inside. I am fully present.

Work and Identity

Distinguishing between work and identity is not easy... if even possible. Of course, making no distinction at all is also problematic. Integration is different than enmeshment.

Those at the extremes get all the press. Working non-stop, convinced of one's indispensable significance, and completely unaware of the fragile house of cards being built to sustain one's sense of worth. At the other end of the spectrum are those who trudge off to the job they hate; loyally and/or begrudgingly put in their time; all the while waiting until it's over each week so they can get back to living.

Where are the wide open spaces in between, where work is an expression of one's identity without being the keystone? Where are the people living their lives at work as much as they are at home or at play, and how are they finding their way? Talk to me.

Dressing Up

I don't usually wear a suit and tie, but there's something about dressing so sharp on the outside that makes me feel quite a bit more sharp on the inside. I'm feeling particularly sharp right now.

I might even dress up more often. Go around impressing myself. Be intimidated by my own presence.

Don't let me near a tux!

Wanderings

Borrowed phrases drift across the expansive steppes of unexplored imaginings. Not at home in my own body. Yet to be introduced to my own soul. Roaming in search of God knows what. I keep coming across abandoned tents and can't help but wonder what everyone knows that I don't. What are the secrets I hear whispered in the wind?

While certainly a foreigner, I am no stranger. I am pilgrim

Confronting Reality

I find that holding certain assumptions can result in avoiding certain realities. The assumptions may be reasonable, but when the outcome is the denial or defiance of developing facts on the ground then those assumptions need to be questioned.

How and when to invest money in the building of my consulting practice is just such a quagmire for me. I assume the investment must decrease the longer it takes to become financially self-sustaining. Time being unquestioned negative feedback about my prospects.

But if the initial estimate of time required was an incorrect assumption, then to interpret what by nature may be a long process negatively is an enormous error. I need to be learning and adjusting as I go. The sooner I learn something, the sooner I can adjust.

Successful living and working requires the willingness to confront reality early and often, think through the implications and make adjustments accordingly. Am I listening?

Practice Practice

I'm reading Dallas Willard. Again.

The connection between the practice of spirituality and the practices of our physical bodies has been of inestimable value to me through the years. Always a fresh challenge. Never a condemning burden.

I need the ongoing challenge. I'm not sure what I do, but somehow I show up in relationships in such a way that no one in my life challenges me. Challenges me to excel, challenges me to grow, challenges me to be more than I am.

Dallas Willard's writings are that challenge to me. A challenge to step to the plate. Assume the mantel of responsibility for my life. Cease minimizing my part in my choices. A challenge to embrace the life that God extends so freely to me.

Any Thoughts?

What are exercises that strengthen one's ability to focus? What processes facilitate transforming valued but neglected "shoulds" into driving and schedule dominating priorities? What means lead to increasing self-awareness—especially of unmet needs that sabotage intentions and undermine one's capacity to choose well in their quest for acknowledgment and legitimacy? Any thoughts?

Relative Reflections

The value of an occasional look into the mirror depends on our capacity to accept what is revealed. I know there are days when I come to the mirror looking for certain things and not wanting to see other things. Either extreme can cause me to see what is not really there and to miss what is staring me in the face.

There are two ways to have a poor self-image. One is to hold deep negative beliefs about yourself. These deep beliefs provide our filter for interpreting reality and guess what? "Reality," as we have misconstructed it, keeps confirming our negative ideas.

The other is to fear that something negative might be true of you. Consequently all your energy goes into maintaining a strong public persona. In this scenario "reality" always gets interpreted positively, and you always come out looking good. Except that you have just cut yourself off from any chance to learn from mistakes, enlist the help of others, relax and be human (read be imperfect).

So on the one hand, it can be a wise reality check to take an occasional look in the mirror. Unless, that is, you have found other ways to adjust what you see.

Moody Man

Temperamental swings take their toll on previously sound foundations. The subtle pressure over time chips away at moorings established over years of faithfulness. Subtle, subtle. Take note now. Choose differently today. Time can be both friend and foe. Each step has significance. Each step is life. My life

Shifting Attention

Corporate mumblings about someone needing to take the fall. Action is necessary even though no one really understands what happened. Lack of response would be interpreted as incompetence, though, any incompetence was what allowed this situation to get to this point in the first place. Now that power is watching, the appearances must be otherwise. The criteria for the next crucial decision is self-protective. The strategy is to shift blame. The motivation is fear. The rewards are self-congratulatory. Nothing changes.

One Brick at a Time

Walls are built one brick at a time. Initially the bricks along the ground are a mere nuisance. We trip occasionally, stub our toe and curse vainly. Imperceptibly the wall grows and poses more of an obstacle and hindrance. Until finally, one day, all we can see is the wall. We are suddenly alone and strangely surprised by this situation. Where did this wall come from? When did it grow so high? How did this happen to me?

If only we had noticed each time we laid a brick down. One brick is easier to remove than an entire wall.

So What Do I Want?

Wanting something bad enough. Isn't that what much of will power is about? Wanting something so much that action, even unpleasant action, is taken. Can the inverse be said for lack of action?

Then there is the problem of our wanters being fundamentally broken somehow. Those of us in the Christian tradition sentimentally term this original sin. My wanter is not even turned on. Or at least not turned on when anyone is looking. I don't have permission to want. That lack of permission is so deeply ingrained, I have trouble identifying what I want. (Fortunately, no one asks.) (Even more fortunately, I am starting to ask.)

Being unclear about what I want versus what others think I should want versus what I need versus what others want and need… results in inaction. I need to get clear on what I want. Not because my wants supercede all other factors, but because only when I am clear about my own wants can I more sensibly and

caringly sort between and integrate the many
and competing voices that cry for my attention.

Dancing at Work

Dancing has been an on-going metaphor of life and work for me. There's an element of technique, but it's the passion invested that gives it its power and joy. I can't help smiling from ear to ear when I dance. I'm engaged, I'm free, I'm expressive, I'm fully myself.

And so it is when working at what one loves. The joy is in the exertion. To hold back is to miss out. Trying to fit in is not to fit at all. It's when everyone stops wondering what the others are thinking about our "moves", that the dance floor comes alive, and the whole is more vibrant and impact-full that the sum of the parts.

I'm going to "work" now. Beware of getting in my way. You might find yourself drawn into the dance!

Firmer Ground of Being

Challenges to the internal illusions
Carefully mastered to shelter the emerging soul.
Authentic, centered confidence stages a daring
  coup
Only to reel at the unsubstantiated yet
  irrefutable accusation
Of being but the next illusion.
Disenfranchised from being
By my own brokenness.
Airtight circle of words
Floating isolated over the jagged terrain of my
  next choice.

That they betray in the courts of conformity
Makes them neither friend nor foe.
Elusive voices who both teach and deceive.
I make my peace with the damning
  uncertainties
And give myself to those who will ultimately
  destroy me.
Firmer ground of being.

Though I die,

More truly have I lived.

True to Who I Am

Unexpected tensions arise, drawing attention to dark, mysterious places where I have not yet trod. Where I do not venture because I have either not acknowledged the existence of such places or not believed I would survive if I swam in such murky waters. But what if the waters are dark not because of some external danger that lurks in their deeps, but because I am not present to bring what light, however weak or strong, I have to offer? The waters will always be dark and fearsome until I wade in and be true to who I am.

Untested Ideal

Sometimes it is easier to complain about not being picked for the team, than it is to get in a situation where one would actually have to step to the plate. When left out by the choice of others, our contribution remains an untapped ideal in our minds. We can feel the disenfranchised victim and leave the precious ideal untested. When we do find or create an opportunity to step to the plate, our contribution then goes from conceptual ideal to concrete reality. And most likely, however adequate, this participation will fall short of the ideal. Even excellence can feel like failure when compared to an ideal. Better to stay out of those situations altogether. Better to keep trying out for teams for which one will never be selected. The ideal will remain intact. That is if the safety of hitting home runs in your imagination is better than the risks of striking out on the ground. It's time for me to risk more strike outs.

⊙⌇⊚—

Rejection Imaginings

Resistance to rejection, real or imagined. One understandable, one less so. Both my world. Love to help people. Hate to sell. One holy. One profane. Such harsh, rigid, unforgiving lines. Such a dangerous world to navigate I've created. Crash or soar. Bless or exploit. Embraced or shunned. Save me.

My Keys to Making Progress

Health and structure. Two areas of personal development that keep coming back to haunt me. I say "haunt" because I am not reminding myself of their importance, but am being reminded by the way they keep popping up in my story as significant keys to my future progress.

Significant roadblocks in the mean time as well. And hence the importance—even urgency—of decoding the cryptogram of my mysterious resistance to concerted action.

Sensitive without Caring

We all know people at either end of the spectrum. Those who march to the beat of their own drummers, impervious to and possibly even unaware of the opinions, needs, and feelings of others. Then there are those who measure their very value by the opinions, needs and feelings of others. We aren't very sure what these people think, because they style their communication by gauging their listener. We all, of course, fall somewhere more complexly in between.

The question it raises is how to be sensitive to others without caring how they respond to us. When I care too deeply about how I might be received, I give others power that I then find sabotaging my own confidence. When I don't care at all, I function in the dark and in a vacuum, and end up harming as many people as I help. Being sensitive to others does not necessarily mean experiencing negative feelings in response to their negative reactions. It just means understanding them objectively and compassionately, and incorporating those insights into the facts that inform my choices. I am then free to modify my choices as a gift to the relationship without either feeling forced to modify my choices in order to protect myself or ignore others completely in order to be myself. Big difference.

Validation

A need I've spent too many years trying to wish away is my need for validation. I don't know what my resistance to external forms of corroboration is about. From one perspective, there is wisdom in a good reality check. In another sense, though, it feels like all legitimizing powers belong to others. Like I need permission to proceed.

Perhaps the fallacious permission language arises from where I look for validation not that I look for validation. When I desire validation in someone else's eyes, I am inadvertently accepting their beliefs and values over my own. I give away my power. Diminished responsibility always undermines dignity. Not good.

If I remain the responsible party, then validating or conflicting evidence is nothing more than valuable data for enhancing my stewardship. I remain in charge and

empowered to make my next decision,
however difficult, however unusual. Good stuff.

Excuse or Shame

Looking for new ways to work on my weaknesses besides beating myself up for having them in the first place.

The extremes of shaming myself (where there is no room for being less than perfect) and excusing myself (where there is room for everything except demanding a higher standard from myself), aren't serving me well. I need something new. Something more like a compassionate self-challenge. Understanding of both the complexities of my foibles and the inestimable value of growing through them.

I know, somewhere way down deep that I cannot yet access, that someone healthier, stronger, more vibrant, poised and decisive is emerging. Part of me can't wait to meet him and has been very busy removing all obstacles to his arrival. Part of me is nervous, maybe threatened, by these changes, and has been masterfully sabotaging the preparation efforts.

If I could only get these two guys to realize they're on the same team.

Exile of Isolation

I may feel alone, but I am not alone. By that I mean I am not alone in my aloneness.

I am not as different as I may like to think. My isolation is shared by many. We are a generation where vast numbers of us walk anonymously among the throngs. Frenzied activity experienced by many, shared by few.

Key for me is acknowledging that what I thought was unique to me and increased my distance from others, ironically could be the very point of connection that could draw me closer to others.

The itinerant who reaches over and touches those he meets along the way. In those touches binding himself with unseen cords in a web of connection no building could contain, no language could categorize, no power could threaten, no organization could encompass.

My own exile notwithstanding, the promised land could be as close as the reach of one's fingertips.

Storied Soul

Poignant stories resonate and reverberate at undiscovered depths of being. Themes beyond words wrap themselves around my soul and teach me subtle variations on the party line. Every day I must dare again to be me. More often than not I am met by quashing, taming efforts that do not trust that the wild, free me will be a force for good. It gets old through the years. Until, that is, I hear another story. Another story where I recognize myself anew.

Simple Directive

The stop sign's directive is clear. A momentary denial of freedom ensures the exercise of freedom for another 500 yards. Survival need not always cost a lot.

There comes a time, though, when there are so many stop signs that life itself has come to a halt. A predicament as debilitating as a crippling crash and as reckless as ignoring the signs outright. There is more than one way to go through life in a coma.

Showing Up Me

I control how I show up in the world.

I heard this turn of words for the first time a couple of weeks ago and find it helpful. While there is much in my context that is out of my control, the manner in which I am personally present always is.

It causes me to reflect on my internal sense of poise, peace and confidence. How much feels authentic and how much feels forced on me by pressures I feel from my context. Not as many good models or standards out there as I would have preferred. Hence the importance of living into my own standards and never being anything less than fully me. It's the least I can do for myself and for those I care about.

Too Transparent

The problem with being too transparent is that no one can see you. We expose too much and people see only the exposure. Instead of revealing to know and be known, (which places an extremely high value on this precious information and consequently is only feasible with a very few people on a rare basis), we reveal to be accepted and congratulated for the bravery transparency requires (which places an extremely low value on this precious information, and we broadcast to as many people and as often as possible.) I consider the latter emotional exhibitionism. I'm not suggesting we go back to wearing social masks. But transparency is not a virtue for its own sake. There are levels and dimensions of self revelation that are appropriate and inappropriate for different sorts of relationships and that accomplish different purposes within those relationships.

Focus, But How?

Where does everything else go when one focuses on one thing alone? Is there some place to tuck the myriad voices that cry out for attention? I suppose if one is absorbed enough in one thing, there is no room for anything else.

So is the task of focus becoming completely filled or becoming completely empty? I imagine some of each depending on how your mind works.

In either case, there is not much practical assistance out there except for stating the obvious. "Be more focused!"

Mastering Anger

Anger doesn't have many constructive outlets. Such potential for such power. So few, though, are masters of what they feel and not the other way around.

I rage inside. Seldom does it break through. Such self-restraint is not mastery either. That I do violence only to my own stomach lining merely limits my impact on others, which I suppose is better than overtly harming them, but hardly accomplishes anything that might benefit them.

There is a responsible, constructive place in the repertoire for anger as a force in the quest to make the world a better place. But we need to become better at feeling it, owning it, and mastering it. Then we will be better positioned to use it. Instead of it using us.

And That's Final

Interrogating the carpet because eye contact is too dangerous, he insists his decision is final. There will be no discussion. What he doesn't realize is that there isn't anyone there with whom to have a discussion. He has evaporated into a positional persona. Jawing an endless series of platitudes and certitudes and justifications and conclusions. Fragile is the authority that must assert itself so vigorously. That must avoid so many vestiges of the human drama. We can protect ourselves from only so many of the unknowns that emerge in all human encounters before we have protected ourselves from having any human encounter. Talk about final!

Death by Suffocation

The worst part of suffocation is remaining conscious. The awareness that you can't get the air you need and the ensuing panic and powerlessness are terrifying.

The point—which is not merely to be morbid for a change of pace—is that suffocation can take many forms. A needy relationship can be suffocating. A job going nowhere can be suffocating. And the consciousness... the awareness that the life is being sucked right out of you can be worse than the controlling relationship or the boring work.

The advantage, if you can call it that, is also the consciousness. That you can see it happening. Maybe see it happening in time to do something about it. Suffocation always ends in death. It is imperative that we do something about it.

Poised for Change

Sudden shifts of direction are hard enough to pull off, much less when one is not already poised on the balls of one's feet. There is an expectancy and preparedness in the tennis player's stance. Too settled translates into too complacent more often than not. Not an issue until the unexpected intrudes and changes the dynamics. The unexpected and changing dynamics are our context. If you haven't come to terms with that fact yet, then every surprise will be a storm. Consequently there is greater peace in poise than in relaxing.

Help Self Help

I find it intriguing that our culture is so smitten with self-improvement efforts. Especially given how slowly people change. I guess I'm admitting I'm old enough to have some experience with the pace of self change.

Intriguing and irrational, but hopeful nonetheless. Despair would be worse. Resignation or fatalism.

No, for all the difficulties involved, I'm glad we err on the side of trying to become healthier and healthier. It speaks to an inner plumb line somewhere within that knows something is amiss. More significantly, it recognizes, even if only dimly, a beauty and fullness that seems to belong to us. If only we could reach a bit further and lay hold of it.

And so we reach. Most all of us reach. I head off into my day now to do some reaching.

Facing Reality

Knowing that something must be done and knowing what must be done are two very different things. Having admitted that I can recognize the obvious, I beg only to confess that I do not chose that which I know. Such a choice would involve some difficult questions. No. The greater need is to find those to whom such questions could be shared. I've discussed these matters with myself for too many years already. The problem is both that I struggle alone and that I am left alone to struggle.

Some hear the word, "struggle" as a sad word. "I am sorry to hear that you are struggling." Others hear the word almost heroically. "I admire the tenacity with which you struggle." My only real commitment to myself is to view life heroically. Hence I am more frustrated about not being a skilled struggler than I am about having struggles.

Interesting the predicaments our frames on reality create for us. We might best be served by facing this reality first.

Present Day Haunting

Traditionally haunting is associated with the lingering ghosts of those who die with unfinished business. Somewhat less fantastically, I find myself haunted by my own unfinished business.

Projects, waiting for attention and hidden unobtrusively at the bottom of the pile, subtly apply an unrelenting pressure like so many bricks balanced precariously on my shoulder.

The relief, of course, comes through action. But such a straightforward, simple principle naively overlooks the dominant reality of the mysterious and complex recesses of my psyche where few dare to tread and comprehension consistently defies all.

I suppose it comes down to how badly I want the haunting to end. Which is worse? Sitting down to the task or carrying the bricks? Yes, many choices for me come down to deciding between negatives, which, interestingly enough, may be an important clue for facilitating

change. What am I completing the project for?
What is the positive, construction outcome that
will be the fruit of the follow through? More
than the reduction of the haunting, I may
derive action-propelling motivation from the
prospect of the completed business.

Self Sabotage

Have you ever wondered whose side you were on? I've always assumed I'd at least be for me. So I'm surprised when I find myself the cause of my own undermining. Self sabotage is different than having weaknesses, lacking skills, or making mistakes. It is a deliberate (if unconscious) working against something you, at the same time, are working for. No excuse will suffice. No other perpetrators on whom to lay the blame.

I need to get all of me on the same team here. It's okay if different aspects of me play different roles on the team. I've already come to terms with the fact that I am more complex than I had expected. But it would sure be nice if we (that is, all of me) at least could agree that we wanted to win the game.

Center of Attention

Maybe it's just that I like to be the center of attention. So content for so many years with understandings of generosity and humility that didn't include room for me, it's awkward to comes to terms with my delight with the limelight. Not that I'm awash with limelight. Hardly. But inside. Part of me is wanting to move front and center. It's time. Not at anyone else's expense. It's simply time to step onto the court and get into the game with an intensity that I have not yet.

Want It Enough

If the route to what one wants goes through territory filled with much that one does not want, what then?

Talking Back to Myself

It's one thing to talk to myself—one of my favorite pastimes. More recently, though, I've found it necessary to talk back to myself. I try my best to maintain a respectful tone. But when I catch myself nodding like a wide-eyed child to the outlandish insinuations fear whispers in my ear, it's all I can do to resist breaking out the whipping noodles.

"Do my eyes deceive me?" I retort to the vaguely familiar stranger in the mirror. "Did you really just travel all the way from articulate professional to stuttering novice in the span of one afternoon?"

I've been persuaded by enough friends that the "castigate, humiliate and beat up on myself" strategy for fostering maturing change hasn't been serving me that well. Command and control efforts like "Stop it!" and "Grow up!" haven't produced much in the way of results either.

So I've taken to putting a friendly arm around my own shoulder (less effective in public where not everyone knows it's impolite to stare), and gently, though directly, asking, "Hey buddy, what do you think is going on here?"

"I'm not here to evaluate or judge. Just making myself available to listen and help you think through some of your, shall we say, less than rational behaviors."

I'll let you know how it goes.

I Don't Know

I don't know.

Not so much a confession as a statement of fact.

If I moved from not knowing I don't know to knowing I don't know, that would be a confession. I can now acknowledge what previously eluded my awareness. There is no shame in the confession. How certain realities remain hidden or cleverly camouflaged is complex and different for each of us. That we should be blessed enough or open enough to learn along the way is cause for exuberant expressions of gratitude. Never shame.

As a statement of fact, I merely reveal autobiographical information. Today, I would like you to know that I don't know.

Slap on the Face

Some lessons in life repeatedly receive the polite nod of assent and the subsequent dismissal into distracted forgetfulness. Not until reality stings us with a jarring slap on the face do we take pause and consider change.

While related, mental assent and life change are two different animals. The health and capabilities of the heart and will are as important as the health and capabilities of one's mind. It seems to me we have lost access to much of what might strengthen our wills and hearts. So many of us wandering from mistake to mistake. Until by consequence or grace we receive a jarring slap on the face.

Lower Center of Gravity

Maybe just a metaphor for maturity. I can feel the difference, though. When I do all the work in my head—make sense of complex dynamics, maintain my self-esteem, justify, rationalize, defend, plan, summon courage, discipline will, focus efforts, be sensitive to others, assert myself, etc. etc.—I'm literally and figuratively top heavy. All my energy has to go toward simply not tipping over.

As I've matured through the years, I have either intentionally or circumstantially become more at home with much of life's perplexities and my own peculiarities. The freeing and refreshing outcome of which I experience as a lower center of gravity. A poise born out of inner strength, depth, richness, and soundness, rather than a persona sustained by constant vigilance, effort, juggling, and performance.

I've come a long ways. I have a long ways yet to go. Feeling the steadiness, flexibility and peace of a lower center of gravity I am emboldened to embrace the journey.

An Extra Measure

An extra measure of the spirit pays an unexpected visit, leaving a more centered clarity in its wake. No precipitating development… quite the contrary. With circumstances escalating that would normally undermine, tap into deep fears, or knock me off balance, I stand both within myself and outside myself. Comfortably both experiencing the dynamic and watching the dynamic. Strangely safe while much is at stake. Not needing to expend my energy holding on so tightly to what is not really mine. All I can think is an extra measure of the spirit.

Seething on the Inside

Seething on the inside with no means of outward expression. A tortuous quandary where anger and power and will collide. The mature find ways to be strong and wise and forceful without being coercive or violent. But so many others flounder between humiliating impotence, punishing rage or a twisted moral avoidance. Those whose wills partner with their anger exert enormous influence and change the world for the better. The rest of us slowly (or not so slowly) destroy ourselves and/or those around us. I guess you could say we change the world as well. Seething on the inside, maybe. But really we must be changing the world for good.

Big Dreams

Does one need permission to dream big? And if so, from whom?

Some seem limitless in their capacity to dream on unbounded scales. Some consider dreams a luxury the practical realities of this life do not afford us.

I refer not to those dreams which serve as an escape from reality, but those which serve as a precursor to reality. Down to earth people for whom dreams are but the initial schematic drawings of a down to earth future which has yet to take form.

I want to be one of those people. That much in my imagination does not currently exist, has no bearing on its potential to exist. Hence the danger of a permission mentality. I, in essence, give a vote to those who cannot yet see or understand what I see. Vetoed by the status quo—norms whose only normality is the ongoing absence of workable alternatives.

The question is not who will affirm me, but who will help me. Others are not life's referees, blowing the whistle and stopping the action when I break the rules, but my teammates and my partners, who are co-creating and advancing the future we have dreamed must now take form.

Conceit or Confidence

The Olympic spirit seems to have few admirers in the media. The inwardly focused athlete is deemed unfriendly and self-absorbed for not giving chatty interviews, smiling enough or waving appreciatively. Anyone who doesn't show up for practice is labeled arrogant and probably doomed to the fate they deserve (which generally is assumed not to include the medal podium.)

This morning I read one reporter wonder aloud whether such behaviors were conceit or confidence. To those of us on the sidelines, I think the question is a speculative, useless and even meaningless line of inquiry. To the competing athlete, though, I imagine its significance lies in how grounded in reality his or her perception of him or herself is.

To know with some accuracy what one needs to do to perform at the top of one's game and to proceed to do just that, however it makes the rest of us feel, is to be admired in my book. On the other hand, an inaccurately too lofty or too low ability assessment is a recipe for trouble. Not for its moral implications in the eyes of others, but simply because the decisions being made concerning focus or practice or late night parties are not grounded in the facts. When it comes to performance competition, it's the facts that get tested.

Ambition and Fear

My ambitions and fears are not friends—yet.
They sabotage and threaten instead of inform
and complement one another. The lack of trust
is palpable—a murky fog distorting the senses,
undermining the decisive next step.
Adversaries inexplicably sworn to discredit the
other. I don't know whether I'm so much
trapped in the middle or somehow playing the
middle. Resolving to an extreme is not an
option. A new way of holding them together in
tension is my task. Encourage them to listen to
each other, partner and collaborate.

Self Talk

Sometimes we have to be our own cheerleader. Especially when we pursue something others are not yet seeing or understanding. We have to remind ourselves of the whys and wherefores of our conviction that we do in fact see something. We have to develop the capacity to discern between the many voices that accuse so "lovingly" of our craziness or naiveté.

Courage flags for many reasons. Not everyone has an Arwyn in their life whispering bold assertions of destinies fulfilled. We learn to whisper to ourselves. Tentatively at first. Almost embarrassed at the audacity and self-centeredness of the exercise. It is not long, though, that we learn our survival depends upon it.

Exploring Motivations

Exploring motivations that are complex and numerous. Not with the intent to resolve or purify, but merely to understand. Understanding offering power to choose more intentionally. To increase in wisdom as one moves toward one's ambitions, instead of one's ambitions magnifying the foolishness of such focused blindness. Such values are not vague niceties for the politely devout, but the anxious realizations of the wounded desperate.

One's capacity to love freely is handicapped by lack of self awareness. Pure motivations are not a prerequisite to powerful love. But ignorance of what colors our choices can be nothing but dangerous.

Increasingly Myself

In knowing and understanding who I am, some forms of knowledge cannot be expressed in words. Cannot be reduced to words. I cannot be reduced to words.

I settle into myself. Like getting comfortable wearing a new suit that is a fresh yet surprisingly fitting expression of who I am.

It still surprises me to discover how good it feels to don new aspects of me as if for the first time and discover they are not awkward appendages. How good it feels to be increasingly me.

Autumn

Winding up and winding down. Autumn is officially upon us. With school starting and so many people back from their summer holidays, much is beginning. Time to refocus, look ahead, dig in. At the same time, with Fall comes the transition to Winter and the end of the year. The final lap before we reach the traditional measuring anniversary of December 31st. Last chance to affect the composition of the photograph that will most certainly be taken, if not by us, then by others. Did we succeed or fail? Learn anything?

I see in Autumn's dual nature not a choice but a tension. A tension between looking forward and looking back. Winding up and winding down. These are not opposites. Some things need to wind down in order for something new to begin. We do not have to ransom the future to the past in order to learn from the past and possibly change the future. Winding up and winding down belong together.

Someone is Me

Taking control of me. A simple statement of owned responsibility on the one hand. A life long process of maturing on the other. Specifically, I'm talking about being willful and intentional.

That I am responsible does not mean I am able. New skills may need to be developed. New patterns may need to be instilled. But someone needs to chose those things. That someone is me.

Habit Forming

Establishing new habits seems to require an odd combination of desire, will, practice, will, need, will, determination, and, yes, will. In instances where the will is weak, any new practice feels like a herculean task, a overwhelming burden, or some dreaded form of self-torture.

The method where the will is expected to dominate and subject all other needs, feelings and desires to it's strict rule, doesn't work very well. I suspect that if there were a way to structure a conversation (yes, within myself), where my needs, fears, desires and will could all take turns listening to each other, I'd be more successful navigating change. Instead of my needs feeling voiceless or maybe even never fully articulated and consequently fighting for attention or exploding unexpected at the most inconvenient moment, they could be acknowledged as real and honored as significant even if not deferred to as controlling.

The task of my will is then no longer to battle in order to win a war, but to coordinate in order to execute a decision.

Podcaster Insight

I was at a podcasting convention recently. (Yes, audioKarl is coming.) Much is happening in this new, but fast developing world of self-published content. Needless to say I learned a lot.

More significant than the technical learning, though, was the conversation with one guy who had his own video podcast on repairing computers. His publishing breakthrough came when he learned not to take himself too seriously.

Not the lesson I was expecting. Certainly not the lesson for which I drove all the way to Ontario. But even as he spoke, I sensed this was a gift message arranged by another and especially for me. Somehow and in some way too much is at stake as I offer my services (sell myself) to those I know… as I move toward speaking and publishing my ideas for more public consumption. But I am not at stake. I'm simply quirky ol' Karl—an enigma in many ways to be sure—but no more and no less than me.

I could feel myself relax inside even as I absorbed this stranger's story. And to think, I almost walked right past that guy. There's just no telling where the next blessing might emerge.

Risk's Sweet Reward

Man, I love to be the center of attention. Not a spectacle, per se. But up front, on, performing. Coming off a speaking event, I am full of the alive feeling of absolutely having to rise to the occasion and meet the moment. Sweet.

Many associate such feelings with vanity, hubris, arrogance. To the extent such worrisome adjectives may be partially true of me, I am not too concerned at the moment. Because dominant is the achievement, the crucial aspect of my role, the encounter with the unknown and unanticipatable dynamics, and the adrenaline rush of risking failure on a moment by moment basis in the presence of others.

Too Cautious?

The visor successfully deflected the glare, but at what expense? We protect ourselves from one danger and blind ourselves to the next. Smothered in an overprotective blanket of cautions and precautions, we lose some of the agility that walking through the minefield demanded. We give ourselves an exhaustive list of all the things at which we should not look, and our attention is filled, but not as we had intended. Avoiding one thing is not necessarily embracing another. What fills the void?

Soul Etchings

Some moments are etched deep within. Their ongoing impact out of proportion with their actual power.

The scars need not be disfiguring or incapacitating, though. How we take our traumas forward—both the good ones and the bad—is a choice. Not an easy choice, but a choice nonetheless. While forever changed, no verdict but our own will determine to what extent the change enriched or damaged.

Preaching to Myself

Pushing for renewed focus. Grasping for the wherewithal to execute. The bias toward action that I preach to others, I want for myself.

Too comfortable in the world of ideas. The problem not being the world of ideas and my utter delight there, but in the "too comfortable."

Complicit

Power's cryptic secrets taunt from a mythical center to which access has been denied. As long as I am willing to cooperate with the governing story, I am complicit in my own marginalization. I hold out my hands and then complain they are shackled.

Pursuing the suspicion there are other stories— or even writing a new one—is a more tumultuous struggle and often a heretical scandal until ultimately validated. Validated or discredited, evaluative conclusions no one is qualified to make.

And yet I must choose my path even if blazing a new one. And there are not many days given within which to accomplish so much learning and doing. Too few to cede the agenda to hesitation.

Something I Must Do

Inhaling deep wafts of the morning mist, I push my way into the day—that now familiar mix of courage and impotence coloring each step.

Foreign are the airs of self assurance that others seem to wear so effortlessly. But I press forward. Destiny's beckoning promise continues to visit in the night, dancing gracefully along the horizon of my imagination. My appreciation for this encouraging angel erases every suggestion that she is but a teasing whore. I am different. I am different for a reason. I am different because I have something to do. I have something I must do.

⟡–

PERSPECTIVE

Climbing to better vantage points.

When standing at the bottom of a chasm, the way forward seems clear enough. That is until I realize that I'm standing at the bottom of a chasm. It's a matter of perspective.

If I believe I am seeing the entire picture, then I am reasonably confident about my alternatives. If I have reason to believe that I am seeing only a small portion of a much larger and more complex terrain, I look for ways to climb to higher ground. I need more and better perspectives in order to make a responsible decision.

The wise person knows that s/he doesn't ever have the entire picture. The wise person is always trying to get to better vantage points, look from a variety of angles, see through other eyes, and obtain additional information.

Life is full of surprises. They can catch us off guard or they can teach us.

Listen in as I scramble for a better perspective.

Centered or Focused?

I lose steam when I lack focus. The lack of clarity is a hindrance. I've been complaining lately of the difficulty of maintaining focus.

I am beginning to suspect, though, that of greater significance is that I am not centered.

Feeling centered is different that feeling focused. I can be centered whether or not I am focused: enjoy a low center of gravity, internal poise, know who I am and whom I serve. Being centered speaks to a soundness and strength within myself. Being focused sees with clarity and steadiness what needs to happen outside of myself.

I think what I'm realizing is that becoming a more centered person comes before becoming a more focused person. While both are essential, one builds on the other. Centeredness extends the reach of my focus.

Moments

Great richness is found in learning to be attentive to moments. They come. They go. When we are present, attentive and engaged they are the experience of fullness itself. When we are busy, distracted, or stressed, they bloom and pass without anyone to enjoy their beauty. There is a poverty of spirit that ensues when we hurry past too many moments. What is a moment? Be attentive and find out. You will never be the same.

Unexpected Gifts

Gifts can be wildly fun to receive. Especially unexpected ones. The best are when someone has been listening and acts on some insight they received in the process. The unsolicited initiative expended on one's behalf fills one's sails with wind.

Gifts can be awkward. Especially because I am not as giving. In that case, though, my attention has shifted off the gift giver and onto myself. Gifts and giving get misconstrued when the focus is misplaced.

I'm learning to enjoy receiving gifts as much as I do giving them.

Strong Convictions

I can't decide whether strongly held convictions inspire or frighten me more. The underlying arrogance of the, "I'm right and you're wrong," starting point of any conversation is troubling for what a unilateral power grab such an assumption represents. On the other hand, the insipid passivity of withdrawing from the conversation altogether in the name of tolerance or relativity or respect smacks too much of excuse-making and conflict avoidance.

Where is that bracing edge where conviction and inquiry, passion and hospitality, living boldly and learning humbly mingle, if not comfortably, then constructively? The stakes are so high when it comes to matters of life and family and work that the conversation absolutely must, regardless of the dangers, be engaged, with all welcome and none retreating.

Diving Into the Day

I am going into this day open to new things. I am making myself available to learn and see differently. I will not let self-protective concerns consume my consciousness. I will not be content to stand on the sideline, but will fill the newly freed space with dance. Out of the security of my own centered presence, I will be able to see and enjoy others–for their own sake and not merely in terms of how they compare to me. I will lay aside measuring and judging. I will embrace honesty and integrity. I will not beat myself up for my weaknesses, nor will I stay quiet about my strengths. I dive headlong into the day, throwing in a playful twist just for fun.

Relentless Time

I can't believe the year is gone. That series of moments labeled 2005 that was my life is done. Is done being labeled 2005, at least. Time's relentless march forward need not be a merciless one. Failures redeemed, milestones achieved, difficulties transcended, the mundane newly appreciated. Richness upon richness. The story continues to be told and enacted, complete with new twists in the plot, unexpected heroes and villains, and no shortage of tears, inspirations, and disappointments. Today marks an ending of sorts. Tomorrow a beginning.

Catapult(ed)

There is both something explosively powerful
and dangerously out of control about the image
of a catapult. Much of the distinction lies in
where you see yourself in the metaphor. Many
years have I worked to develop and hone skills
of loading, aiming and mastering the catapult
only to recognize more recently myself hurling
through the air, arms and legs flailing
desperately. Little control of my own. Still a
lot of power involved. A major impact almost
assured, though the same cannot be said of my
personal survival.

It's not a question looking for resolution.
Simply an image that teases out some of the
tensions inherent in trying to live boldly.

Sensing Change

I'm sensing change in the air. The morning fog weighs heavy on the breeze rustling through. There is something irrepressible about the wind, though, and my lips part in a relieved smile.

That change is coming is good to be aware and prepared. Discerning what change is coming is another matter altogether. I don't have a sense of that yet.

So with heightened senses I embark on my day, seeing the world through fresh eyes. But maybe it is not the world around me that has changed. Maybe it is I who am changing. How does one prepare for that?

When It Counts

There is a readiness to do what needs to be done that I find very attractive that is in direct contrast to how I feel about things like training, discipline and practicing. Key then may be finding connections to what is attractive and making those central to my framing of any discipline undertaken.

The readiness to do what needs to be done.

Reliance Unaware

Amazing how we count on certain things. This morning it is the telephone that has gone from invisible amenity to focal nuisance. Static loud enough to drown out all but the faintest inkling of what might be a human voice at the other end. We sit around the answering machine and take wild stabs at recognizing the identity of the caller. The content of the message we don't even bother with. We answer the phone as if we were an answering machine, mechanically notifying each caller that we are going to hang up on them and call back on a different phone.

Fortunately the phone company agrees that the situation is intolerable (a refreshing contrast to software companies) and will be out tomorrow to repair the lines. Which brings me back to the observation, that we count on certain things. Functioning phones being one of them. We have incorporated into our way of being the assumption that we can make contact and be contacted when and where we need. A reliable benefit that far outweighs the risk of occasional isolation. What I find so interesting is how off guard I'm caught when that on which I relied fails. It's not the failure that surprises, but the invisibility of that which I have taken for granted.

It's freeing to have things like phones move off the radar screen because of their reliability. But what about people? Or God? Have the reliable and faithful in my life become invisible? I'd hate to think that the only way to get my attention was to fail me.

Eyes of Fear

How much of life do we live through the lens of fear? How dangerous are our relationships, our jobs, are we ourselves?

How often do we perceive legitimate criticisms of our work as attacks? How often do we conceal our desires out of concern not to be accused of selfishness? How many slights do we silently incur lest any protest be misread?

Opportunities for strengthening communication, building trust and deepening levels of maturity—albeit difficult ones—slip through our fingers when we react through the eyes of fear.

I'm preaching to myself, of course. One of the many lessons of life we learn more slowly than we would have hoped in retrospect. But we do not live in retrospect. We live and learn moving forward. So I do not need to waste time judging my mistakes, (like living through the lens of fear,) when I can more fulfillingly

expend my effort learning to live through a
lens of love.

Exploring vs. Wandering

Blurred at best is any distinction between exploring and wandering. Between blazing a new path and being lost. Am I the determined, persistent visionary courageously co-creating the emerging future or the deluded, disoriented egoist possessed by my own unconscious needs? Both extremes, granted. But useful. To pursue the first there is the risk of the second.

Key seems to be locating points of reference one can interact with without being absorbed by. Good friends can serve here well. The combination of love and loyalty creates a safe dynamic for working through much that is mysterious in life. Jesus would be another such a point of reference for me. (Not though in the conservative tendency to defer unthinkingly to some 21st century theological conceptualization of morality or obedience or faithfulness.)

One thing have I determined: I will not fail to explore in order to avoid the risk of wandering. I will not reduce my efforts to participate in the future in order to console myself or anyone else that I am not dishonoring the past.

Non Sense

It never ceases to amaze my jaded sensibilities how such understated exaggerations of blatant subtlety find a way to position themselves with suspiciously audacious humility at the center of attention. I must not see clearly for the perspectives that swirl with unfocused clarity cloud the certainties with fresh insights that teach me that I do not know. Adolescent outrageousness and conviction-void tolerance entrench themselves as the new orthodoxy, from which no deviance will be tolerated and all transgressions will be punished. Be careful to be yourself unless you're not like me then be yourself like I would if I were you. Let me tell you that, whatever you do, don't let anyone else tell you what to do. I'm beginning to see now, as long I as don't insist on realizing anything that is less than an authentic expression of myself and by which no one else would ever find offense. I am free. I am empty. I am alone.

Getting Perspective

Stepping away may be necessary to gain some perspective. We can get too close to our own choices. We lose track of the destinations for which we are enduring each step and get lost along the way. We miss the future disoriented by the present. Conversely, we might be so focused on a dream conjured early in the journey that we fail to learn from the clues life's bumps and jolts provide. Lessons that might have served to inform and refine the dream. We miss the present in service of the future. Either way we are not serving ourselves well. Either way finding ways to step back and get some perspective is essential.

Going Back to Go Forward

Sometimes going forward requires going back. I'm loathe to admit it, but my buddy makes a pressing case.

I hate going back. Feels like I don't have what it takes to go forward. Or that I lost my way and have to retrace my steps. But what if I left something I need behind? Wouldn't it be as wise as it would be necessary to retrieve it?

And which is worse, admitting that I'm lost or never arriving at my hoped for destination? How can I have what it takes if I'm not willing to discover its name and go out and get it?

And if any of these things are located somewhere along life's journey where I have already climbed, which of the Ten Commandments asserts, "Thou shalt not tread where thou hast trod before?" Base camps are not revisited because of failure, but because of the demands of the trek.

Sometimes going forward requires going back.

Clouds of Ambiguity

The approaching storm clouds bear portents of ambiguity. Destructive downpour or replenishing bounty. Too much or not enough. All at once or in measured portion. Feeding floods or flowers. The dark skies thunder in their absolute power and make neither promise nor threat. And yet.

It has been said, "Expect the best. Prepare for the worst." It is a fine line, though, between pragmatism and paranoia. Whether we are grounded in hope in a broken world, or operate out of fear in a world full of possibilities. We can look into the turbulent skies and say, "Thank you," or "Why me?"

It's worth a moment of reflection. It will make a world of difference when you are either digging yourself out of the mud or arranging a gorgeous bouquet of fresh cut flowers. While either scenario may be your tomorrow, neither resolves the ambiguity within which we either hope or despair.

Costly Misreading

Opposition on multiple fronts. Confusion misread as antagonism.

No companions for the journey. Leadership misread as isolation.

The burden of proof remains on me. Challenge misread as burden.

New bruises and scars daily. Learning misread as failure.

Refusing to give up. Stewardship misread as denial.

Mustering the will to choose again. Growth opportunity misread as discouragement.

Death. Vindication misread as judgment.

What Will Be

What will be will be. I used to consider such attitudes a form of giving up. But I sense as much, if not more, peace than passivity in this phrase today. A peace that does not bother with passivity because we are a part of something bigger than ourselves. Something going on whether or not we participate. Someone building something wonderful to which our contribution is a significant enhancement but not the foundation itself.

And so the sun will again rise in the morning. It will shine whether I achieve or fail. Failure finally loses its vicious grip on my psyche. I actually become willing to be play a bigger part in the story as I realize how small I am in the overall picture.

Refreshing Mist

Cool mist blankets weary faces in the predawn stillness. "Another day!" being either a shout of anticipation or a groan of despair. Chesterton's child-like God delighted again each morning with another miraculous cycle. Ever the same, always new. Or the sinking realization that one's waking did not end the nightmare, but, in fact, seems to be closing in all around you, sealing off all exits.

We take ourselves wherever we go. Gift or curse, depending on one's frame of reference. Human maturity is imperceptibly slow. A reflection of steady, sure progress or stubborn resistance?

There's something refreshing about the morning mist, though, that cleanses spirits and renews hope. Got to get outside earlier in the day and lift my weary face upward in receptive anticipation.

Conversation of One

Conversations in motion. Undulating landscapes manipulate without polarity or dimension. Mornings are but rumors that assault clearer visions by reducing them to words. One can only be reduced so many times a week before it takes a toll. Systematically penalized for being other than the hero of the community fairy tale. So is rolling out of bed a cowardly sell out or a defiant act of courage? How to even cope with the suspicion that one is living a different story line than everyone else. Reality in flux. A new conversation. Sadly still a conversation of one.

Coloring Books

No one asks permission to color outside the lines.

One either cooperates with the structure provided or one doesn't. The lines are there for a reason. We waste our energy resenting them.

There is a season when it is helpful and we are willing to express ourselves within the given structure. At some point, though, we can no longer express ourselves, contribute ourselves, be ourselves within the lines drawn by others. Life's contours are framed by those who dare to color freely, boldly, authentically. We fail both ourselves and the world when we do not enrich and inform and extend those contours with our own distinct strokes.

We learn life by coloring within the lines. We come alive when we color outside the lines.

⟡⟐—

Words Give Pause

Time, energy and creativity are precious commodities. I'd probably juxtapose them with whim, inertia and formula.

I certainly desire to apply them with intention, wisdom and love. The trick is making the desire more than just so many words. How much of my time, energy and creativity would people describe as characterized by intention, wisdom and love?

Whim, inertia and formula, on the other hand, reflect a sort of wastefulness, if not outright disregard, for what is most valuable even to me. A form of being disoriented while believing one is perfectly oriented. On track, but no longer aware of which track. Riding the latest wave without acknowledging the underlying tidal currents.

Time, energy, creativity.

Intention, wisdom, love.

Words over which to pause.

Absence versus Presence

While certainly the absence of disease and dysfunction, what is health the presence of? We are much better at defining what many things are not rather than what they are. We know in excruciating detail what morality is the absence of, but can we say much about what it is the presence of? What about peace? Same problem. Justice? Ethics? Marriage? Life?

We trudge through life with much to avoid and a myriad of voices asserting what we need to prevent. But can we articulate what we are trying to create? Just because I am moving away from something negative does not mean I am moving toward something positive. I'm not hearing many positive, constructive, alternative visions of life being placed on the table for consideration. Seems like a treasure trove of opportunity.

So Obvious?

Tamper-proof renditions of the world
   according to
The next self-appointed guardian of circular
   truths
Whoever that may be.

The names hardly matter any more,
The modus operandi are
All the same.

Our eyes are clear, objective and strong.
Any applause corroborates the veracity of our
   creed.
Any persecution validates the threat such truth
   poses.

All others are
Fools to be mocked
Villains to be opposed or
Partisans to be dismissed.

It gets so old.
The evangelical preacher, the gay activist, the

liberal academic, the conservative talk show host,
The union representative, the gun enthusiast, the vegan, the home-schooler, the border vigilante.

Will we ever learn?

It seems so obvious to me.

Context Matters

Overcast skies block both the sun's life-giving light and the its energy-draining heat. Here at summer's apex, the unexpected cloud cover counts a welcome blessing. I'm sure during winter's reign all prayers are for their dispersal.

The clouds themselves are neither friend nor foe. Context affects the lenses through which we filter reality.

I wonder what seasonal attributes I carry into this day.

Dream Work

Busy day ahead. Three writing projects to complete. I decided that instead of interpreting the pressure negatively, I needed to realize that I'm living my dream. So in a very real sense, such a day is a dream come true.

And, of course, what is a dream day except one begun with one's blog. Excuse me now. I have some "work" to do.

Turn of Phrase

The potential and
Limitations of
Words.

Both powerful.
Neither definitive.
Meaning flows where interpretation's
 boundaries
Stand to resist.

The not yet imagined frontiers of creation and
The crippling diminishment of the human soul
Both
Either

On a turn of phrase.

Informing Clues

What if the distractions that I assumed were confusing me were actually clues available to guide me? They catch my eye because they contain a glimmer of something attractive to me, even if they themselves are not what I am either looking for or need. But as a clue, instead of an answer, there may be much worth paying attention to.

Maybe it is the quest for answers where we get off track. Answers relieve of responsibility, and we know that is not possible. Clues inform the responsible without drawing conclusions or forcing decisions. I need to be more intentional about my own openness to the clues that I find strewn along my path.

Repertoire of Frames

Wealth and poverty bind the human spirit. It need not be so. Both in their stark reality-bending consequences for those who cope at the edges, and as insidious frames of reference in which those of us who are neither rich nor poor are oddly content to limit ourselves.

I'm thinking about myself—as usual—and not the world's financially destitute. Wondering how I manage to keep slipping into such a limiting, constricting poverty mentality as I paradoxically explore new frontiers of personal and professional contribution.

So many crucial investments placed out of reach by my own zero-sum mindset. I perceive an absence of options simply because I cannot find a rainforest in the desert. But the desert is infinitely rich and diverse once freed form the rainforest frame of reference.

I need a wider repertoire of frames.

Fabricated Stress

Pressure fabricated in one's own imagination. Stressing that which was never the case. How often? The wasted energy. The lost time. The internal toll.

Can't second guess so much, but do need to take a step back every so often. Make sure I am perceiving with some perspective. It's when certain things fill the canvas, perspective and periphery get eliminated. Makes it more difficult to interpret the subject.

Clues Everywhere

Even silhouettes can betray demeanor. The recesses of light's absence as revealing as its presence. Clues everywhere. Where are the attending eyes? One would assume at least the curious or desperate would show up.

Short-sighted or possibly overwhelmed, we abruptly give up at the perimeter of perceived reality and consequently cede its interpretation to others. We feel powerless and/or victimized within the confines of that interpretation, but never come to terms with the mortal blow we dealt ourselves by standing at the periphery working only with what we are handed. How often does our own passivity become our most active weapon against ourselves?

Majoring in the Majors

Ideas, relationships and processes are my majors.

My drive and passion are highest when I'm immersed in a major.

Two thoughts come to mind. How can I major in my majors and minor in my minors, when it all needs to happen? How can I establish more conscious and emotional connections between my minors and how they get me to my majors.

On the first count, there are, of course, people for whom my minors are their majors. People for whom, what I avoid they pursue; what sucks the life out of me infuses them with meaning and purpose; what is a stretch or a chore for me comes easily and delightfully to them. I need not travel alone. Who do I need on my team?

On the second count, I imagine that if I could see more clearly how the roles and tasks I don't want to do will get me to what I do want to do, then some motivational determination and energy will follow. An assumption, to be sure, but not without basis.

I need more ways to tap into my majors and supplement my minors, so that my internal resources aren't exhausted trying to become something I'm not in order to some day be who I am. Tragic irony to lay the tracks but forget the destination.

Tamper Proof

A lot of people out there defending tamper-proof world views. Striving to define reality correctly rather than navigate it responsibly. It is the difference between getting it right versus getting it alive. Do we need to be photographers who capture everything in the scene as accurately as possible in order to understand how to best live in that scene? Or do we need to become the co-authors of an ever-emerging, never-stationary, always-embodied experience which becomes real only as we make each choice along the way?

Such choices do not take place in a vacuum. The choices of those who have gone before provide valuable resources from which we can develop compasses, maps, directional and warning signs. It is when we step away from our own culpability in the development of the human story, that those compasses and maps become tamper-proof world views. Instead of insightful clues helping us craft a more meaningful future, they become blinding manuals that reduce the future to awkward encores of the past.

As I have said on other occasions, I find myself willing to risk getting it wrong in order to get it more alive.

Wrinkles, Sigh

A wrinkle is seldom celebrated. Whether it be a new line under your eye or a crease in the sharp button-down you just pressed, wrinkles are, more often than not, spoilers. We ultimately have to accept them… come to terms with their presence… and learn to move on. But the fact is, their advent doesn't make anyone smile.

A wrinkle in the plans means not that they have been changed, but only that they have been impacted. How the impact plays itself out in altered arrangements remains to be worked through. Hence the ambivalence and unease when encountering a wrinkle. Far from a disaster, but if a blessing, quite disguised. Her mother-in-law's unannounced visit put a wrinkle in her weekend plans.

We build our dreams. We prioritize our goals. We organize our days. With wrinkles we cope.

Lop-Sided Belonging

Belonging involves compromise. The terms of belonging, though, are weighted in the hands of any group's existing insiders. Most, if not all, of the work of compromise is consequently borne by the newcomer—the one in the least secure position in the new relationship. A problematic situation at best.

We even have vocabulary to describe the difficulty of "breaking in" to a new community. As if walls without doorways encircled and protected these clusters.

A few do manage to succeed in the double responsibility of breaking in and compromising, but at what cost? Not only does the group fallaciously interpret these exceptions as evidence of their generous openness, and proceed to harden in their unyielding standards of acceptance; but new members are immediately diminished by the lop-sided give-without-take concessions wrung from their greater need to belong.

The mutuality inherent in relationship and compromise needs courageous advocates within organizations, communities and cliques to risk the changes required to facilitate both. Every new member changes a group completely.

Discovering the New World

Casting about for moorings that steady without binding. When the journey feels more like drifting than traveling. There are not many points of reference out in the middle of the ocean. There is not much room for exploration tied securely to the dock.

We used to think the world was flat. We used to think the universe revolved around the earth. Of what are we currently certain, which we mistakenly trust as a reliable point of reference? By which we miss the mark by aiming, not merely in the wrong direction, but in the wrong dimension. For which we are not merely mistaken, but unaware, without vocabulary or frame of reference.

It is a new day. It is a new world.

Being Present Today

In all the plans and preparations for our tomorrows, we can only live our today. We each live our todays at across a wide spectrum of intentionality, awareness and appreciation. Even as we make current sacrifices for the sake of what is yet to emerge, no day consists merely of the absence of what we would have preferred. The mistake some of us make is when we allow our sacrifice for the sake of the future absorb so much of our attention that we do not see, experience, or enter into the presence of what our today does in fact consist. "When I finish this degree, then…" "When I am making X number of dollars, then…" We miss the today that we have in hand dwelling on the tomorrow that is just out of reach.

Liminal Unrealities

I grope my way through some sort of liminal space. It's feeling like it's been a long time. It's been years. I'm open to whatever the new normal might be like. I just want to be there already. What I suspect, though, is that the new normal will not be any version of normal at all. Learning to function on that side of the threshold may not involve being functional at all. Learning to navigate may not involve progress or orientation or directions. And if an arrival of some sorts at a "place" where I get to stay for a while isn't in the cards, I at least hope the dynamic of this richer, deeper, more mature reality feels like home. I'm still feeling my way around. I'm pretty sure I've a long ways to go.

Always Learning

For learning to happen, one's capacity to change must be flexible if not expanding. Strength not being the issue so much as stretching. Life is not something we perfect and get right, but something we learn and grow into gradually. Nor is life an ideal concept we experience imperfectly, but an imperfect experience we can talk about conceptually.

Interestingly enough, life on the ground is a stretching enterprise. (Unless, of course, you are one of those for whom life is a pretty straight-forward matter; which would then bring the total number up to ONE!) Could there be something in the design intentionally structured around learning?

Poker Woes

I must say poker isn't nearly as fun to play when one spends a good portion of the night losing. Between the cards, the cards and the cards, I didn't stand a chance. It's almost worse than losing as a result of my own poor judgment. I didn't even get the satisfaction of beating up on myself.

It's amazing how little it helps to remind oneself that it's just a game. As the others' laughter gets louder and their conversation more animated, I can feel myself slumping inwardly (and probably outwardly), unable to share in the joy. My eyes focus in on the cards in my hand as if by staring with enough intensity they will switch suits or my missing fourth deuce will suddenly turn up.

I manage a smile and a few salutary words of congratulations. I'm a big boy now and rise to such occasions. And besides, I'm supremely confident that next time the outcomes will be very different. I can't wait.

Taking But a Step

Step by step rather than all at once. Each step having its own value without the whole being at stake. When it's all or nothing, even the smallest action holds enormous risk. It's like accepting ultimate responsibility all of the time just by agreeing to get out of bed in the morning. So much cannot stand or fall with one.

Step by step is something at once, even if not everything. Whereas all at once is nothing until the whole is achieved.

Step by step provides not only progress with each step but learning. The whole becomes better informed and more wisely designed in the process itself.

Step by step. Courage for the next step.

Living the Day I Choose

It's pouring rain outside. Cleansing, nourishing blessing? Messy, dangerous nuisance? Depends on one's perspective.

I have been learning a lot recently about my power and responsibility when interpreting reality. I will have a better experience of today if I choose to welcome the rainfall rather than curse it. (Knowing I'm a native Angeleno, you can probably guess my first tendency.)

What alternate interpretations are there for the myriad other things that happen during the course of a day? What is my role in how they affect me? How will my choices affect those very circumstances, people and events? Do I influence change by trying to get others to change? Or do I merely show up differently myself which becomes the next event they need to respond to? A choice possibly different than what they would have chosen had I not made my choice to be different. Hence change. Change without manipulation or control.

I believe I am beginning to like the rain.

True North

Always new skills to learn. Every day a new world to navigate. We take our eyes off the road for a moment, and the traffic stopped for everyone but us. We return from any detour, not to the interstate, but to a different map of the universe. Each corner we turn becomes a change in dimension rather than a change in direction. A world where compasses find true north in the complexities of the human heart, and the heart is as reliable as it is not.

What are these skills we need to learn for such disorienting times? What is our responsibility in shaping the world we inhabit? Are we waiting for the scientists or theologians or politicians to decide for us? I hope not. We dare not. But the question remains on the table.

Connecting vs. Networking

The thing about connections, interestingly enough, is the connecting. I think about the people with whom I feel a personal connection and I get happy. When I think about business networking, I think about getting strangers to like or respect me and get stressed. I need to think about networking the way I experience connecting. Simply, that I'm out and about looking for those with whom I might have a connection. Translated… enjoy a relationship. Instead of a negative, stressful duty, networking might become an attractive, interesting highlight.

Thanks to my associates with whom I enjoy connecting so much!

Filtered Focus

Across the length of our living room spreads an oriental carpet. Its intricate design would be dizzying except that it coalesces and, to the casual eye, presents itself as a whole.

My eyes cannot appreciate detail unless they first comprehend the whole. Some people cannot see the whole until their eyes have taken in all the details of which it is comprised.

Sometimes intricate and involved pieces come across busy or noisy, and consequently annoy or distract instead of unify. Alternately, a complicated background can quite effectively set off and help focus the eyes on what deserves attention in the foreground.

It's all a matter of where the eye is drawn. Sometimes it can be as important to intentionally trigger people's filters as it is to direct their focus. What do you notice first when you enter a room?

⟳

Self Reminder

I'm following my own advice. Imagine that.

"Many challenges. No excuses."

If I want to see change I need to start with myself.

Easier said than done in times of frustration, high need, or when weary. That's when I need a reminder.

Long Odds

We don't pursue our dreams because we like
the odds. Neither do we achieve them by
ignoring the odds. When few share our visions,
it becomes all the more important that we bring
to the world what has been given (possibly
uniquely) to us to see. When few understand
what we are trying to accomplish, the odds
mount against us. The critique of doubters and
cynics acts as quenching poison for which we
must find our antidote. The benevolent, albeit
blank stares of most require we offer a new
vocabulary with which to introduce our new
world. To turn a blind eye to the reasons
underlying the long odds will be as fatal as it is
negligent.

Winning Ideas

Everyone seems to move so quickly. They say there are no new ideas out there. But I must say it is additionally frustrating to see ideas I am working on take off elsewhere just as I'm developing them. Such is our world. We must press forward. Make our respective contributions. Let the flow of events and the multiple trajectories of creativity emerge onto the today into which yesterday I was planning as my tomorrow, and in light of which I must already adjust as my past.

I must say, though, that there is also the desire to win. Something about being first, seen, recognized, rewarded. To be a part of something incredible, influential, helpful and world-changing. To have high-school students assigned essays about what would the world be like if Karl hadn't made his contribution to the workplace culture revolution.

We'll leave it to others to debate whether we're on a flight of self-absorbed vanity or a determined trek toward fulfilling our destiny. I, for my part, must live my day.

Challenge and Remind

Pausing to be present with my words. To sit
among them and let them dance around me. To
watch as new worlds emerge and melt away.
New ideas challenge the very underpinnings of
reality and then remind me that love has
always been the answer. New adventures, old
lessons. New territory, old terrain.

Holiday Focus

Holiday focus. How's that for an oxymoron?!

Kids off school, I've got lots of work on my plate. Making time to enjoy each other. Keeping on task in my unstructured world. Expectations all around. Resisting the tendency to make other people's happiness my responsibility. Trying to enjoy the both/and (an uneasy tension) without slipping into either/or (a simplistic resolution.) Smiles and stress, chores and parties, joy and obligations. It all becomes a blur. It's a good blur this year. In coming to terms with the "reason for the season," it's nice to be free from the need to pretend like we're focusing on the reason for the season. I'm planning on enjoying Christmas in all it's unfocused messiness!

Attitude

Attitude is momentum fuel.

Dousing flames with gasoline. Intangible powers unleashed.

Whether arising spontaneously or out of meticulous training, my attitude colors everything. Whether intentional choice or circumstantial mood, it is the difference between trudging along and dancing freely. Raging forest fire or controlled burn. Destructive blaze or warming hearth. Terrifying threat or sustaining passion.

Attitude for this next day of my life. What will I choose?

Sharp Corners

When our kids were small we attached plastic cushions to the corners of our coffee table. Inevitably their toddling would become tumbling, and those sharp corners would inflict serious damage. It was ours to foresee what they were too young and inexperienced to foresee for themselves.

As adults we can see many of life's sharp corners before we stumble into them, and adjust accordingly. But what about when we spot someone running head long into a fire or tottering dangerously close to the edge of the cliff? If we see something that someone else does not yet see—for whatever reason—is it not our responsibility to do something beneficial with that knowledge? To withhold it and then announce after the disaster, "I could see that coming," seems negligent. To then blame them for their lack of foresight, however foolish, seems cruel.

Friendship has always called for some form of having each others' backs. Not all eyes are clear enough to see all life's sharp corners.

Valuable Boundaries

We limit our driving to one side of the street not because we need to be restrained, but because we share the road with others. Both to facilitate flow and to prevent accidents.

So it is in all of life. Boundaries serve to enhance effectiveness and protect against harm. When the limits and boundaries are established by others, especially those in positions of authority, we too easily forget their purpose and redirect our attention to our relationship with the authorities. When we need to question or reject certain authorities, we make the mistake of rejecting the life-serving boundaries as well as the persons, offices, and/or institutions. We validate the idiom by "throwing the baby out with the bath water."

The value of boundaries in life is inestimable. Their purpose, place and design deserves renewed attention for its own sake. The problem of authority abused and authority misapplied deserves attention as well. But as a different subject. Not as a rationale for demanding the freedom to drive on both sides of the road.

Firsts

Nerves, pressure, excitement, stress, performance, achievement, failure, gift, embarrassment, emerge, soar. A lot of different angles on another day at work. But it's not just another day at work. It's a first. And I'm excited and nervous at the same time. It's going to be a good day.

Blurred Edges

When the room starts to spin and there is nothing to hold onto; when the outline of the once familiar blurs beyond recognition and bleeds across dimensions; when the mosaic keeps rearranging itself, and, instead of finding the new perspectives helpful, we merely keep finding them. The silent scream is invalidated before it can be noticed. Death's icy embrace and other strangleholds we give ourselves to… lurk and haunt and hold out promises they cannot keep. Why am I so often deceived?

What if the spinning and blurred edges were actually the beginnings of seeing more accurately? That what I have assumed to be healthy is the lie, and to return to a stable, sharply focused experience would be to seal the door on the tomb, forever locking myself in a cramped, though self-justifying world. The darkness reframed as our all-encompassing orthodoxy. The familiarity with which we are

certain about each "fact" masking the fact that
we are, in fact, dead.

Ebb and Flow

I'm taken with how life changes even while it stays the same. Like the ever changing, always constant river.

This morning I'm thinking the ebb and flow of relationships. New friends that I'm excited about. Old friends who are moving away. I think I'm getting better at going with the flow. Accepting the reality of periodic loss and making the internal adjustments necessary to thrive going forward.

I think for a season there, I believed the alternatives were connection or isolation. But, the facts seem to evidence a coming and going of various sorts of connections. Some merely social brushes past each other. Some task-based collaborations. A few more intimate friendships. Some where we share only words. Some where we share only work. Some where we share life.

And this variety is good. I need neither to keep everyone at arm's length nor become everyone's best friend. Ebb and flow. Ever changing. Always the same.

Background Music

The thing about background music is that it plays a supporting role. It enhances the environment without drawing attention to itself. Rather than becoming the experience, it complements the experience. No one stops what they're doing to hum along, fantasize about their concert debut, or inquire into the title or original performer.

In not being noticed background music finds its applause. Anonymity distinguishes it from the competition. Its success is measured by the fruit of those whom it serves.

I would imagine something similar is true for people as well. We would be mistaken to underestimate the significance of those whose presence and efforts enhance the effectiveness of others. Who are these people in your life?

Navigating New Territory

The thing about hiking in new territory is that even if the destination is visible from one's current vantage point, the route there isn't. There are no telling what twists and turns, slopes and ravines, rushing rivers, wild animals, or non-negotiable dead ends lie between here and there. We may start out with one course in mind, but from the next vantage point realize that we must adjust course radically in order to ultimately reach our desired destination. Such adjustments can feel like set-backs or a failure to accurately chart the initial course. In fact, though, we are encountering the simple realities of foreign terrain, which by its very nature is an on-going learning experience. The failure would be not to learn and adjust. That our actual path was not the one we had first set out on or hoped to have traveled must remain secondary to our determination to reach our destination.

Return on Investment

I'm learning to think differently about return on investment.

The difference relates to the use of time. What return on investment do I get on my time?

Those who know me best know my short attention span for many tasks, the lack of structure in my working world, and the seemingly random bursts of inspiration and productivity that characterizes my output.

It obviously wouldn't work for me to evaluate all time the same. Two hours of "unproductive" space may result in thirty minutes of incredible insights and writing productivity. Whereas, if I tried to sit down and be creative at a scheduled time, it might take me five or six hours to produce an equivalent outcome.

Hence the usefulness of thinking in terms of return on investment. My focus shifts away from measuring levels of effort or busyness to selecting best paths for achieving desired outcomes; from what I'm putting into my efforts to what I'm getting out of my efforts.

A big difference.

DECISION-MAKING

Getting off the sidelines and into the game.

There is a time for watching the game from the sidelines. To learn the rules, to hone one's skills, and to get the big picture. At some point, though, we need to join the game.

At some point we have to make decisions, choose between alternatives, take action, commit. We can't reflect forever. We can't gather all the information that might help us make the perfect decision. Life doesn't wait.

At some point we have to put ourselves out there. At some point we have to show up and engage. Most certainly before we feel fully prepared.

Listen in as I try to get out of my head and into motion on the ground.

⟶

No Excuses

Fundamentally my success in life depends on adhering to the maxim, "no excuses." Yes, all people and most circumstances are outside of my control. So many factors and dynamics influencing and impacting each contour in the path I tread. Nevertheless, however complicated my next step may be, it is I who must take it.

"I wish I could have taken this other route that someone else took, or made such and such a choice that was available last year, or faced fewer obstacles or had less clowns working around me or ogres above me." Wishful thinking. Incontestably and unverifiably true on the one hand, but in simple denial of the facts and the realities of the choices not being made on the other.

When it comes right down to it, I have no excuses. I am responsible for what I can do and must do it, whether easy or difficult, straightforward or complicated, delightful or painful, energizing or draining. No excuses.

Decisions in Motion

Decisions that result in action. Concrete and measurable. The advantage of which is not to pass judgment and move on, but to evaluate efficacy, learn and make the next decision.

Structure's New Disciple

Structure has the potential to both empower and stultify. I currently need its more empowering properties. I've spent so many years resisting its constricting, conformist dangers, that I'm finding it not so easy to embrace or appropriate its undergirding and fortifying strengths.

Flooded with options and decisions at every turn, I find myself paralyzed in a multi-dimensional maze, where I not only have to choose which way to turn, but chose to keep making that choice against all others as well. No path has its own boundaries that limit the range of choices available. A living nightmare where the possibility of anything at all becomes the reality of nothing in particular.

Needless to say I have become a quick study on the merits of structure.

Dive In

Enough testing the waters—dive in. Life's too short. Opportunities pass too quickly. Some things cannot be learned loitering along the shoreline.

Something Has Got to Change

Something has got to change. I have to change something.

When current methods, strategies and practices aren't serving us well, how much damage—or lack of progress—are we willing to sustain before coming to terms with the fact that we have to do something differently? No need to minimize the existence or impact of the many factors outside of our control. But ultimately we all must, and specifically now I must, look deep and hard at what I need to change.

To plug along in the name of commitment, perseverance or determination in the face of consistently contradictory facts is neither commitment, perseverance nor determination.

The challenge becomes how to give up on failing methods, strategies and practices without giving up on the dream one is working toward. We must garner the courage to face what isn't working, and instead of interpreting it as failure or weakness, seizing it as a powerful learning opportunity. The need to change, even if it comes in the form of emergency sirens or howling pain, is a gift to be embraced not a indictment to be avoided.

Talking Less, Living More

It comes down to choices. Making a decision and living the decision.

Research, reflection, and discussion are valuable only insofar as they inform an eventual enacted choice.

Sometimes it seems that people are content to talk and think. It's all noise to me these days. In fact, I'd rather engage with a person who acted without thinking before anyone who thinks without acting.

I'm a recovering thinker myself. Scary the dimensions and depths into which my mind delightedly loiters. The question is whether or not all the processing is leading to richer, fuller, sounder, more loving living. At issue is not processing less, but choosing more.

Embracing change, experimenting with new behaviors, getting involved with others, giving form to faithfulness. Turning creeds into cups of cold water, turning dreams into plans of action, turning personal values into personal

change, turning general expectations into
specific requests. There's only one command.
It involves making a decision to do something.

Diving In

Catapulting new ideas over the barriers of fear, resistance and tunnel vision. Experiments in otherness. Assuming frameworks that do not yet exist. Testing the waters, not by sticking a toe in, but by diving in. Commentary and demands be damned.

Not a very sensitive course of action, but sensitivity is not one of my main concerns these days. I'm already too sensitive if anything. Time to forge ahead with more purpose, intention and aggressiveness. In the inseparable tension between reflection and action, I'm ramping up the action.

Emotion Ambush

It's interesting how powerful our emotions are. Actually, I should say, I'm repeatedly both caught off guard and frustrated by how easily and how often I am ambushed in my decision-making by feelings out of proportion with the facts. A blessing and a curse. Adding flavor, texture and rhythm for so much. What varies, though, depending on my own internal health, is whether they are enhancing additions or distorting additions. A mixed bag at best.

Back in the Saddle 1

Back in the saddle after some time off. Grateful for play and rest and changes in routine. Adjusting back to focus, schedules and to-do lists. The accountability of projects and cash flow requirements. The internal push to connect and reconnect, write and rewrite, create and recreate. It's good to be away. It's good to be back.

Back in the Saddle 2

It feels like I've been ignoring a close friend. Dwelling in this special, yet unusual space, letting words spill from a full heart into a formless text field. Was I crazy to allow such a treasure to be crowded out?!

I watch the clock even as I strive to write freely. My first appointment of the day crowding my psyche already.

So be it. Better to set down a few words of pent up desire, than to postpone yet again, waiting for a more luxurious moment to emerge. Not every path in the forest leads to a spacious clearing.

Blah, Blah, Blah

Dry, brittle iterations of last year's formula for health, wealth and happiness. Blah, blah, blah. So many talkers. So many content with words.

When did words shift from being descriptors of reality to substitutes for reality? When did visions go from being vivid images that inspired energetic co-creation of the future to dogmatic recitations of a prescripted story line?

Words have power when they call into being that which was previously but an idea. "Let there be light." A blessing. A promise.

Words that float and hover with no responsible grounding in the complex intricacies of life are deceptive and dangerous and result in outcomes like violent strategies for achieving peace and justice in the world; marriage vows binding people to abusive and/or vacuous relationships; leadership practices that reduce people to their skills, talents, and gifts (i.e. usefulness) in order to build a company or a church or any of a number of noble causes.

Blah, blah, blah. Ya think? Tell me something I don't already know. Whatever. The signs of verbal fatigue are everywhere. And then there are those words humanity has never quite been able to shake: "Do unto others…"

Focus and Push

Time to focus and push. Good projects. Exciting directions. Concrete initiatives. Let's do it. Time to make it happen. Happen in a concerted, concentrated way.

No excuses. In spite of fears. In the face of disbelief. Undeterred by any obstacle. Facing down all opposition.

It is time. Focus and push.

Deciding What's Important

Deciding what is important to me. While we've already established I don't have access to know what I want, important to me might be doable.

Having said that, I do realize that what I say is important to me is often contradicted by what I do. A good look at my schedule is a sobering reality check.

The gap between intent and outcome acknowledged, I suspect there is fruit to be born in articulating and rearticulating, sorting and resorting, committing and recommitting to all that is most important to me. As the pressures of this crazy world taunt and tempt and squeeze and compete, I have in effect established my own criteria for making decisions. Having decided what is most important provides a reflective framework for making decisions about much that remains. Now, what is important to me?

Restored Routines

Normally I would associate myself with those who eschew routines of any sort. I like things new and different. I bore easily of patterns. But in this season where I have no patterns or schedules, I welcome the return to the school routine this morning. Up early. Trying to finish my shower before the hot water runs out. A too-quick breakfast. Shuttling the kids to two different schools. Settling down over a hot cup of coffee with my blog. Nothing like the absence of structure to help one appreciate the value of structure.

Do It

Life always comes down to one's choices as they manifest themselves on the ground. For all the benefits of being able to talk about life, life is not lived until it is enacted.

New Habits

I want to be different. Change some things. It probably has to do with forming some new habits. New ways of being that serve me better. Choices in what I do and when I do it that contribute rather than detract, build instead of chip away at, facilitate focus rather than magnify neglect.

My perennial problem with new habits is the built-in resistance to change that I seemed to have mastered. Or maybe it's wanting something bad enough. Or conversely maybe there's not enough pain and down side to my current practices to motivate me toward something better.

Something needs to change. I need to take a first step now.

Why Postpone the Inevitable?

Following through on old matters today. Amazing how much easier it would have been to have faced these issues when they first arose. Why do we tend to wait until our hand is forced? And depending on one's threshold for pain, it can be quite a while before some of us get to that breaking point. And breaking is exactly what it feels like.

And so maybe I have answered my own question. We may feel we risk breaking if we confront some of these difficult issues. What form the breaking takes is, of course, unknown. But that unknown risk is fearsome enough that we are persuaded to hope, however vainly, that the problem may just resolve itself if we ignore it long enough. Ah, silly man. Postpone action at your own peril. The wise do not so blithely ignore the lessons of past mistakes.

The Stuff of Dreams

Living the dream is not the stuff of dreams.
Grounded, unrelenting effort applied at every
turn. Deliberate even in rest and pause.
Wanting something bad enough so that all
outer obstacles and inner demons are worth
confronting.

We weep only should the dream remain a
dream. Fleshed out in the complexities of lived
life, such visions no doubt lose some luster.
We slog as much as we float. But drudgery,
fear and difficulties are nothing compared to
the slow death promised to those who dream
without living.

When Words Don't Suffice

There comes a point when words no longer suffice. When the language of relationship must find some other form in order to express itself adequately.

Sometimes I can't find words that articulate the depth and complexity of what I'm trying to communicate. While possibly a poverty of vocabulary, I suspect it's more likely the nature of uncharted territory. Such a challenge requires an explorer's courage.

Other times I'm not sure what's worth saying. No topic comes to mind or all topics seem pointless. In order to mean the most, it is vital to say the least. Maybe simply enjoy each others presence.

Words can lose their power when they become disconnected from action. There is a time when one needs to stop talking and start doing, or risk losing credibility. Words don't always suffice.

Enough words for now.

Mercy Calm

The search for peace takes us through a dizzying array of empty promises and seductive turns of phrase. As I have complained on previous occasions, most are far more articulate about what life is the absence of rather than of what it's presence consists. This peace for which I yearn is not a vague spiritual inner calmness, which would be mine for the taking if only I stopped failing at… (You fill in the blank with the religious, metaphysical or special interest group prerequisite of your choice.)

My search… my hope… is for a peace that takes the form of a capacity to make choices. Choices made with neither certainty nor vindication. Only the suspicion, upon which we will bet everything, that at the end of the day, there is mercy.

Road to Nowhere

The road of least resistance may be easy, but it is not always effective. Forget all the promised character building benefits of taking the more difficult route. We miss the point if the intent becomes to make our decision-making criteria finding the most impassable path of all just to prove that we value inner strengthening.

The focus needs to be on outcomes. Which course of action will result in the desired or necessary outcomes? If the desired outcome is safety, then dangerous or harmful behaviors need to be confronted, no matter how unpleasant or difficult. A failure to do so would suggest that one may desire a different outcome, like harmony, for example in this instance.

The focus on achieving outcomes shifts attention to the effectiveness of one's efforts, instead of, however inadvertently, on trying to make one's life easier. Avoiding an unpleasant experience is actually harder to do (and never quite finished) than accomplishing a specific outcome, however difficult. A hard road anywhere is better than an easy road nowhere.

Simple Complexity

Simple insights into complex issues. Not simplifying what is complex, which is a form of denial and avoidance. But approaching what is multi-faceted slowly, thoughtfully, methodically. Layer by layer. Perspective by perspective. Acting while gaining understanding, and not postponing action until achieving understanding. Not needing to master before engaging. May feel slower, but actually one is making progress from the get go.

We hesitate and delay, convincing ourselves we need more and better information before we can make a decision. But there is no way to get complete information and there are no such things as perfect decisions.

We need to make as wise a decision as is possible as early as is possible. Not an easily identifiable benchmark, but a surer route to making progress.

I Wish, or Do I?

Sometimes I wish certain things about work or life were different than they are. All well and good, unless if I believe my best chance for experiencing change is to continue with the wishing.

I have a mug imprinted with the Gandhi quote, "Be the change you wish for wish for the world." Be it. Do it.

Maybe the difference between wishing and hoping is that wishing is passive while hope participates. Wishing desires everything to change around us. Hope lives as though the change has already taken place.

Such a distinction begs the question, "How then do I live?" If you looked at my choices, would you know what sort of world I am hoping for?

Planning to Adjust

I try to hold planning and adjusting in collaborative fraternity. But they weary of each other. The tension is palpable. Another plan butts up against reality and resents the gloating adjustments necessary for moving ahead. It is the goading of the jealous younger sibling, though, since the meanderings of change in a vacuum repeatedly prove that adjusting without a baseline plan against which to work isn't much more than chaos.

Why they do not embrace is a mystery to me. Such natural friends it seems. And yet planning resists any adjustments along the way. Adjusting resents being tied to and constrained by the defining structure of the plan.

I have chosen to foster this rivalry. Eager to exploit the benefits of their separate yet inseparable contributions.

Get Out There

It feels good to put myself out there where the rubber meets the road. Act on the ideas I've been developing for so many years. Test them in the crucible of other peoples' realities. As an outcome of working with me, will people make more and better decisions? Experience a greater sense of peace about the decisions they do make? Come out of hiding and give the gift of themselves to the world? We will see. The initial feedback is good. The only way to find out is to put myself out there.

Subtly Persuasive

Suggestions linger, if not haunt; while assertions are discarded before they are even discredited. The ability to catch someone's attention while looking the other way and leave them wondering whether or not you were flirting—to the extent that they then initiate conversation with you to find resolution—is the goal of persuasive communication.

I do not try to overcome your resistance. I arouse your curiosity. I do not try to reassure your reluctance. I enhance my own mystery. I respect and therefore tap into your own desire to learn and need to change, not my own need for you to agree with or be like me.

It's a matter of on whom I choose to focus. If I am doing something for myself, then I need to compel, force, command, assert, dominate my way upon you, and the risk of your rejection, difference or indifference cannot be permitted. If you are my focus, then I tickle, poke at, accentuate your own learning edges so that you

want to take action and pursue new
possibilities.

Double Doses

Double doses go down hard. The searching for deeper meanings gets old after a while. The responsible next step needs to be chosen. Life in one form or another always continues. We give away power and courage to let circumstances push us around too much. We wonder where the others are before we realize that it's ours to initiate. Whatever is going on around me or to me, I need to show up authentically and unreservedly me.

Dealing

Storm clouds nonchalantly gather like loitering thugs looking for an excuse to explode. The traffic continues to race around me oblivious to the darkening sky. Something tells me an umbrella in tow would be in order.

Life's storms no longer being cause for fear. Facts with which to deal. How well do I deal? Or do I merely wait for the facts to be different than they are? Interesting question. I'm not always sure. It's a certainty that with each passing day I take another step toward death. But do I take another step toward life? Do I passively wish for the traffic to carry me through or the storm clouds to refrain from thundering?

I have long forsworn passivity, but when buffeted by the winds, choosing feels differently.

Bias Toward Action

Act. Do. Live.

I'm far more reflective than I am active. Life has a reflective component, but only insofar as it enhances the choices we make. We need to realize our dreams as much, if not more, than we need to have them.

I need to realize my dreams. I need to enact my life. I need to throw the weight over to making the next decision. I need to operate with a bias toward action.

Busy Day

Where did the day go? Too early for bed, but the anticipation of sinking down into a bottomless pillow and getting lost in a myriad of surrealistic dreams is growing on me.

It was a good day. That is always welcome. Busy. Active. Engaging. Involved. Even in exhaustion I feel more alive than often when rested. That is as it should be. Hard work is good.

Answers vs. Actions

Whether or not an answer is available is always secondary. In order to live, one must continue to choose one's next actions.

I am intrigued by the tendency to look for answers when circumstances don't go as planned. We hear people ranting, "Why did such and such happen? I want answers!" As if knowing this information will do something helpful. All this line of inquiry accomplishes is to take our attention away from where it is especially needed at the moment—on what decision needs to be made next.

Granted, much can be learned from what goes wrong, mistakes, unanticipated turns of events. In such a case, the same criteria applies: we need to identify the decision such information will helpfully inform. If we cannot identify what decision(s) we are trying to make, such inquiries more likely will provide little more than self-satisfying therapeutic indulgences.

I've had much more success when I can keep my focus on making decision and taking action, than in conducting investigations in the search for answers.

Competing Priorities

Valuing multiple priorities while trying to focus on a particular course of action can be crazy-making. No matter how resolutely my eyes fix their gaze on a chosen course of action, my ears hear nothing but the shouts of the outranked priorities. I am continually justifying to myself the merits of my most recent use-of-time decision. Such constant mental gymnastics is exhausting, not to mention distracting and time consuming. What to do with the voices, though? That's the problem. They are persuasive and relentless.

One Step at a Time

Lofty visions inspire impressionable hearts, but the lack of progress down the road is telling. Inspire me to change the world and you change nothing. Inspire me to take my next step, and nothing will be able to stay the same.

Reinforcing New Patterns

Decisions need to be backed with action. Resolve needs to be reinforced with actions.

The best are small steps that serve as a form of practice. A learning process in which we approximate our ultimate goal by supporting, sustaining, and trying it over and over again.

Big shifts rarely happen all at once. We are too unfamiliar with the experience of life in this new realm to excel within it from the beginning. It's like moving to a new country with a radically different culture. We can move physically all at once, but the learning how to live and how to live fully in a fundamentally different world takes time. We not only have to learn how to function within the new structures, but how to think, feel and thrive out of a different framework of being.

And so it is with change on any scale. Making the decision to change is the crucial first step. But finding ways to learn, practice and reinforce that decision are the steps crucial to its ultimate success.

Choices

The most brilliant ideas in the world don't amount to a thing unless they take the form of choices. Concepts certainly help us think more clearly and thoroughly, but by themselves are not life.

My point here is not to denigrate the value of ideas, but to heighten the significance of our choices. We enact life. Engage, participate, do. We are missing much if we merely stand on the sidelines and limit our involvement to thinking and talking.

I know I need to get more involved in playing the game. I know I have some choices to make.

Jolted Awake

Sudden thunderclaps break the reverie, while opaque sheets of water pelt and soak and wash over everything. Startled into alertness, I begrudgingly acknowledge there is something about a storm that gets one's attention.

Remaining alert through the rhythms of life's pressures is an ebb and flow dynamic. I accept responsibility for my own stewardship therein. But storms come nonetheless. No respecter of the responsible are they that break in without warning or purpose. Always it is left to me to choose my response. Jolted awake, no longer in control, I remain a player and must act. And so I greet the storm. I call it by name, neither denying its power nor surrendering my own.

So, now that you have my attention…

Vacation Rhythm

As rare as it is that I listen to my own advice,
I'm off for a week of vacation. Not that I'm
feeling the need for a break in this busy season
of business building, but as a family it is time
to get away together and have some fun. The
kids are off from school, the extended family is
gathering for our annual camping reunion, and
the patterns of seasons and their cycles gift an
underlying rhythm to the routines of daily life.

A Matter of Life and Death

Determination's route from resolve to choices is certainly more perilous than I ever imagined. While the vistas from the top and the satisfaction of the achievement are probably glorious beyond measure, there are so many places where the location of the next toe hold is not apparent, or what you thought would provide a solid grip and hold your weight crumbles in your hand. Injury is a given and falling a real risk. You periodically find yourself question the wisdom of continuing.

The only hope lies at the top. To return to the valley is to choose death by suffocation. To fall along the way is at least death in pursuit of life. And, who knows, it might be life as well.

Uninitiated Lenses

In spite of methodically cautious process I find myself catapulted into an utterly alien realm. Efforts to minimize disruption and chaos don't always succeed as we might have anticipated or hoped. And so my world is new, and my life is new. Accompanying the freshness is a steep learning curve. And even with age visits the challenge to see as through uninitiated lenses.

Discipline and choices and the application of the will in the face of complex and undecipherable struggles within. Alternately at home and a stranger in my own body. Both at peace and restless within my own soul. Shuddering at the possibilities all within reach for both good and evil. The question is less, what will I reach for, as much as it is, will I reach at all.

It is just an assumption that dawn precedes sunset. What if the sunset precedes the dawn?

Structure and Time

Time and structure go hand in hand. I've been learning the hard way.

When the hours of my day are highly structured, I feel imprisoned, constrained, controlled. No space for the imagination to explore, no place for the unexpected to intrude, no room for conversation to deepen or the new to emerge.

I've been surprised to discover that the absence of structure isn't much better. No boundaries to all the possibilities. No deadlines around which to develop priorities. Infinite options available at every moment paralyze instead of empower. The mind bogged down with continually justifying the current use of time against all the others.

So I'm building structure into my day. Enough to focus efforts, prioritize decisions, and make actual progress. Not so much to shut down the creative spaces and interactions I need to function as well. Life, of course, is a learning process. I keep being surprised, though, by where the lessons turn up.

HOPE

Mustering courage for a challenging journey.

The future is unknown. The future is multi-faceted and complex. The future holds as many dangers as it does opportunities.

To hope is to trust that the future is worth exploring. But such trust can be difficult to sustain over a lifetime of bumps and bruises, mishaps and accidents, crimes and tragedies.

I'm learning that hope doesn't arise out of knowing the right answer or doing life correctly. It seems to have much more with being around accepting, supportive, and inspiring people.

Hope sustains my energy levels, holds out a helping hand, undergirds and fortifies, assures of a promised future I may not yet be able to see.

Listen in as I build my repertoire of hope.

Trying Silence

There was a space in the silence
I stepped into
Though I had avoided it until now.

Strange voices speak with familiarity.
I stood my ground.
It may be quiet, but there is no peace.

I weep at the insights
Shudder at the lies
Honestly uncertain which frightens me more.

A home awaits me in the silence
Where the broken and the pure
Share tea and chores and bless each other.

Not sensing a place to rest, I pace
Sorting rumors of death and life
Beckoning from within this new place.

A good-natured laugh breaks in
Reminding me I am not alone in the silence.

I will remain, relax, change.

Bright Crisp Mornings

There's something about the crystal clear freshness of a crisp, bright morning that braces the soul for the inevitable realities of the day. Instead of fatigued dread, though, there is on these mornings spirited anticipation. This is my day. My day that I will seize and mold into something beautiful. Obstacles are not enemies to fear but challenges to confront. Opposition does not portend failure but new partners to win over to success. I feel powerful, grounded, and free. I love bright crisp mornings.

Fullness and Risk

Why are fullness and risk so intertwined? I'm literally exhausted by my efforts to disentangle them. To set fullness apart in a safe, secure place. Easily accessible. Readily available.

No. Inevitably that place is flat and colorless. Sterile. Heat without warmth or the aroma of baking bread.

The experience of fullness accompanies the embrace of risk. The placing of something particularly and especially you out on the table in the high stakes human drama, wagering against all the fears of pain and loss, that the pay off is far richer and more valuable than we've been led to believe.

It is that wager itself that infuses color, adds dimension and intensifies the aroma. Don't tell me for all my efforts that I actually have been working against all I have been longing for.

Moody Clouds

Overcast skies attempt to color the day drab, overwhelming even the sun. Unwittingly I find myself lured into the heavy mood. A bracing face slap later, though, I remember my pledge not to take my cues from outside myself. I set the tone to my day. I choose how I will press into the lifeless grey that surrounds me and infuse my steps with fullness and power. I accept responsibility for the colors and textures on my soul's palette.

So the sun does not join me today. There are other sources of light.

Companions for Courage

There is a fair amount of courage one derives from the courage of others. Or I should say, there is a fair amount of courage I derive when accompanied by the courageous.

I am not talking about the confident. That is a different skill, albeit also an important one. I am talking about a fellowship of mustering. Walking alongside those who have to summon something extra from a deep, inarticulate recess within themselves to accomplish their task. Whether it be to take on a daunting mission or to confront a mean-spirited coworker, the risks (even the irrational ones) are tangible and dangerous.

Hence the mustering. The drawing on deeper, stronger, richer, sounder resources to choose as we know in our heart of hearts we must.

I, for one, am more likely to rise to the courage-mustering task in the company of those who are determined to do so as well.

Courage engenders courage. Fear engenders fear.

Join me.

Please.

Crumbling Fortifications

Crumbling fortifications could spell disaster. Could spell rebirth.

We do not receive all new things with open and grateful arms. Some changes need to break through, force their way in. When life emerges, there is no stopping it. Witness the fragile grass that breaks through asphalt expanses.

I feel that way about maturity sometimes. When I do not see or refuse to face needed change, other forces come into play and the ground shifts beneath me. The terrain itself collapses and unfolds. My fortifications begin to crumble. Suddenly how I feel about change is moot. I either face the reality or deny it. The fact that what served well previously now fails me, need not be interpreted as failure or defeat. Just a fact.

Time to shift focus to what is emerging. Especially if what is emerging is life.

Random Imagining

The peppermint candy cane melts into the steaming chocolate, to which I surrender an almost sensual moan of pleasure. As if the chocolate weren't sweet enough. I step out onto the veranda and take in the morning buzz of a city crawling out of bed. My mind methodically working through the alternatives. Restless dreams suggest a light about to break through the clouds. Or are the clouds about to smother the light? The risks mount even while I stand watching the candy dissolve into swirls of molten allure. The sound of a fist hammering at the door breaks my reverie and my comforting mug shatters at my feet. They are here. I know exactly what I need to do.

Impossible Calm

Thrashing around for a foothold in life's quicksand only exasperates the panic and accelerates the inevitable suffocation. Fear and desperation cloud judgment and choke out reason—like the sinking swimmer who drowns his would be rescuer.

Unable to hear advice shouted from positions of relative safety. Blind to the rescue efforts that failed to head off the disaster in the first place. Everyone else too late and too far away. Again.

Only calm can save him now. From whence will it come?

Deadly Calm

There is a calm as still as death. It is possible
to shut down completely. Walking and
breathing but little more. So safe. No risks. No
adventures. Never a victim. Never a loss. No
skinned knees. No humiliating failures. Yes,
perfectly safe.

Oh yes, and as good as dead. Stillborn in
adulthood.

Where is the calm that stokes life's flames and
thrives in turbulence—that which the ancients
call peace?

I Choose Today

Blindingly blue skies infuse the horizon with a naive freshness that not even the night's jaded hostility can diminish. While darkness smothers the cries of anguish arising from so many parts of the world, dawn continues to stubbornly insist on the possibility of the next day. The story does not end when the night becomes unbearable.

And with morning comes the next set of choices. And once again the human spirit chooses to live. Some spend the day wishing night would not return. Some try to live as if there were no such phenomenon as night or darkness or… loss. But some spend the day reimagining a world where love has an impact on fear and consequently on our capacity to meet the challenges of the darkness.

Who am I when the first rays of tomorrow announce themselves as today? When I finally do push myself out of bed, I am neither naive nor jaded, and therefore must choose who and how I will be today. I will rise and greet the

dawn. I will take the story line in the direction
of hope, even if hope's promise is to be
fulfilled tomorrow.

Hoping for Happiness?

Hope is different than happiness. Obvious?

Not necessarily. We tend to confuse the expected effects of hope with happiness. That somehow to believe that, at the end of the story, all will be well, should result in an upbeat mood for me here in the middle of the story.

Instead of either hope or happiness we get a strange (and frequently irresponsible) reinterpretation of what is transpiring here in the middle of the story. Our part of the story. We either want pain and evil vanquished, and take up arms to that end. The casualties of our righteous hostility lie scattered across the battlefield of our moral crusades. Or we pretend that pain and evil have already been vanquished and any remnant is but a gift from God to test our faith and enhance our characters. What response is there but docile and unquestioning gratitude?

But if pain and evil are harsh realities here in our part of the story (whether or not their ultimate doom is guaranteed), then included in my discipleship responsibilities is a thoughtful, intentional and lifelong response.

I can neither ignore nor be consumed by all that is wrong.

Hope makes it possible for me, in the midst of and in spite of my harsh reality, to function within it and to act creatively to counter it. If my energy is not wasted on denying or demonizing, it can be directed toward healing and restoring. Toward creating a tomorrow more reflective of the reign of the good and just God. The hope that comes from knowing the end of the story sustains and nourishes my spirit in the face of the seemingly insurmountable odds that we face in the middle of the story. Whether or not I find moments of happiness along the way, I give all of myself to living a full and meaningful life because I have hope.

Apprehending Change

Small shifts in uniform gradations like the steady background beat of a warning drum. Relentless and imperceptible, the entire horizon unfolds in a disturbingly miraculous way, reorienting everything within its sweep.

A few sit on the ground, arms crossed, backs to the rising sun, eyes squeezed shut in scandalized rejection of any landscapes not illustrated in the manual. They form a formidable barrier blocking my way forward until I realize that, like it or not, they are part of the landscape as well.

This is a miracle I cannot apprehend.

Practicing Hope

The morning chill threatens to extinguish the fire stoked back to life so recently. Flames are as fragile as they are powerful. A night's sleep can provide needed rest for renewed vigor or a loss of momentum and an opening for fear to creep back in.

It is no small thing that our stories are bounded on all sides by hope. Challenges, difficulties, obstacles, and complexities are significant realities with which life in this broken world confronts us. Hope is a flame fanner. A fire stoker.

We don't need to avoid or fight all that comes against us as much as we need to nurture and practice hope.

The Wind Blows Where It Will

Turbulent winds stir up as much as they sweep away. Hence the risk inherent in walking out in the wind. Is the risk of what might be stirred up worth the potential benefit of what might be cleaned up? One doesn't negotiate with a storm. The last person to give orders to these gusts of pure power was King Lear. We all know how that story ended. The wind is not a nuisance which we can compartmentalize or ignore, but a landscape altering reality with which to come to terms.

It's Not My Job

Even when the shoulds and oughts all belong to someone else, we are never absolved of a duty to act in light of the presenting reality. It may be unfair. It is probably unjust. It almost always painful.

We don't step in and do what they should or ought to have done, as if we could cover or recover what is absent. We enable the negligence with such a course.

We do what is our own personal should or ought. Yes, the unchoices of others impact the context of our next choice. By honoring our own next ought, our shoulds transform into wills and wants. Radical acts of freedom in an otherwise enslaved world. Seldom vindicated but always powerful contributions to hope-drained scenario and scenario.

While others give up, run away, hide, or cover their eyes, we love again. That's our job.

Dawn's Courage

At dawn's first suggestion, discerning the darkness from the fog is no simple task. We inch forward, hoping that we progress forward instead of back, but not really certain. That we choose to move while early is an act of courage. The temptation to wait until the fog burns off is tangible. But the days are growing shorter, and the nights are already too long for complacency. Action is crucial. Decisions are constant. Reflection must be brief. Discernment must be on target. Roused from bed at dawn's first suggestion, we engage with life.

⊙⚬—

Babying My Will

The steaming mug convinces a bare majority
of the fingers gripping it for dear life that
worse things have happened than icy mornings.
A slow, childishly slow, release of the ceramic
vestige of warmth and the mock tears of grief
for the parting of ways takes place as part of a
winter ritual cursing dawn's impotence.

There are needs and shoulds and wants and
musts that drive a harder bargain or threaten
with a bigger stick than body comforts, and so
I muster my will to force that final push out of
the door.

I usually feel stronger after an act of will,
however significant or mundane. It's nice to
have a few less than momentous decisions with
which to experience the power rush of willing
myself to something wise but not necessarily
gratifying. My will needs to get all the strokes
it can to build its courage for the decisions
where more is at stake than shivering fingers.

Frustrated Expectations or Expectant Hope?

What is it with the expectation that life should be smooth, comfortable, and pleasing? More than fallacious thinking, we are failing ourselves and each other by refusing to come to terms with the pervasively broken, pain-filled and complex journey we share with both the suffering poor and the suffering differently wealthy, the marginally good and the delightfully evil, the heroes who sin spectacularly and the corrupt who give so generously, the petty bureaucrat who will not hand you the next form to save his life, but in a crisis will put himself in harm's way to save your life.

It makes no sense at all while we are clinging to the myth of the frictionless ideal. But in the cold, dark, defiled wreckage of a creation at war with itself, the power, activity and intention of someone good can be glimpsed. Instead of the sullied norm, it becomes the glimmer of hope. Rather than the righteous cause which we battle to protect, it is our last chance, our only remaining foothold, the keystone without which all would crumble.

Thank God it all hasn't crumbled.

Symbol Pause

Today we packed up the Christmas decorations. A dried out tree lies in the backyard awaiting its final dismemberment. All the color, every aroma, the rich symbols of advent and incarnation and hope are now cardboard boxes, dust, and fodder for the recycling bin. The glory of the season remains a glory because it does not remain the season. The power of the symbols will revive next year precisely because they were wrapped in newspaper and stashed in the garage this year. We cannot do Advent all year long. Nor Christmas nor Lent nor Easter. All truths all of the time quickly blurs into no truths any of the time. We simply cannot attend to everything always.

As difficult as cleaning up after Christmas is, I smile knowingly when the last ribbon is swept away.

Easter Risings

And so not even death itself could foil the triumph of God in Jesus. Though the forces of darkness and evil continue to wreak havoc and dominate the human story, we pin our hopes on one particular empty tomb and the vindication of God's commitment to his children to which it points.

While possibly surpassed by the incarnation as miracles go, it stands alone in history in the force of its implications for human life and hope. Today is the anniversary of when Jesus made the world safe—not from the presence and effects of evil—but from the judgment of God for being those who tolerate and perpetrate evil.

We find ourselves free to do our living out in the light, without shame or fear, in a spacious realm called grace. So we too rise each day and live the gift which are our lives alongside, under girded and surrounded by the living God.

Driven to Live

From what quarter of the universe do we derive the drive to perform at the top of our game? From deep within? From another dimension altogether? Both/And.

The forces that compel us to press hard and press forward are not all healthy ones, but we do not have the luxury of clearing out all dross before getting out of bed each morning. We can but fix our eyes on the prize that draws us ahead. We engage with our hopes and dreams in the context of our sufferings and circumstances, and don't look back. We trust because our intentions are good that whatever immaturities and brokenness we bring to the journey will be transformed into something new, beautiful and beneficial along the way.

And so back to the original question. From where does the drive to engage fully and participate in life unreservedly come?

⊙⁄⊙—

Dreamers Don't Fit

Someone asked when it would prove unviably unrealistic or outright selfish to pursue my dreams. It's a fallacious question. My dreams are my contribution. If I let them go and choose a path where I fit in and travel with the pack, then I fail both myself and the world. In that scenario, the one thing that distinguishes me would be the one thing that I didn't contribute to the mix. I may as well not be in the mix.

Of course, one man's dreams don't make sense to another. If I see as valuable something that you don't, how do I serve you by keeping the information to myself? Yes, it can be upsetting when someone travels against the flow. It can feel like an unspoken judgment of sorts.

But it is, in fact, a gift. I will not be deterred from giving my gift.

The Stewardship of Decision

Catapulted into another day, I attempt to lay out all the should-do's and want-to-do's and must-do's and decide what will become a done or a think-more-about or a kind-of-do and hopefully not a botch-it.

It's all my life. It's all a gift. I know I've made it clear that I enjoy some of it a lot and some of it not at all. But it is all sacred. The stewardship of decision weighs heavily yet ennobling upon my shoulders. I wouldn't trade it for the world. I wouldn't give it up for the certainty of obedience or the vindication of reward. I willfully and recklessly invest all my hope in the incoercible favor of my maker, the unrestrained fellowship of my savior, and the unverifiable power of my sustainer.

Hmm. To what task shall I next give myself?

Fear's Calibrations

Calibrated down to the facial expressions. The amount of energy required is enormous. What will happen to me? The question haunts and colors everything in fear. The step become softer. The eyes grow tentative. The voice prefaces and qualifies even the most innocuous statement.

Is this even worth showing up for? When one's mere presence is a mere annoyance, an unwelcome disruption.

What courageous frame of reference frees the human soul to be unique in the context of others? When are the distinctions enhancements as opposed to detriments? Certainly the experience of community does not require that we all disappear as individuals.

I am reminded of the apostle John's juxtaposition of fear with love. From whence does my decision to step more softly derive?

Four Word Prayer

Deeper, richer, stronger, sounder.

Words that are prayer for me. I need express nothing else. Further words would only distort and diminish their scope and import. Drag them from the realm of prayer and confine them to tyranny of precise meanings and proper syntax.

Left alone, they steep, infusing flavor, aroma and texture as well as content. They roll around in my mouth and quickly penetrate my being. Each encompasses more than it contains; expresses more than it says; solves more than it resolves.

Deeper, richer, stronger, sounder.

Brave the Grey

Chilled heart braves the grey dawn, wandering in search of what it may already possess. Magnificent gift or audacious grab. Turning off the path, the dew dances around my ankles and the quest loses some urgency in the seductive glories of the moment. Icy winds swoop in with an abrupt reminder that loitering is not safe during the storm season. I pick up my pace and wonder whether obtaining my goal or getting out of the cold is my greater drive. What seemed easily true journeying along lush riverbanks may no longer be the case in the desert. We assume much when we traverse paths blazed by others. Neither the dim grey light nor the harshness of the terrain will steal my courage, though maybe steel my nerve.

Desert Decisions

Temperature rising in the desert. Intensity in the midst of deprivation. Trying to conserve energy with tinges of panic urging a desperate run before it's too late. Identical horizons echo blindness without the darkness. Inaction is not an option. What clues to discerning next steps lie undiscovered deep within?

Stretch

Stretching is both a form of physical exercise and a description of the effort necessary to accomplish what seems out of reach. Which, of course, begs the question: what sorts of exercises exist for the training of the psyche to achieve above and beyond what one's circumstances would suggest possible?

Thanksgiving as Good Practice

Gratitude is a choice. It is also always an available choice. No matter what difficulties buffet our lives, we have the option to identify something (however miniscule) and say thanks. Such a practice actually frees us to concentrate more fully on addressing our difficulties. Set into a context of gratitude, they lose their power to overwhelm or ruin or obsess us. Less afraid we are better poised to deal.

I'm discovering there seems to be a correlation between our practice of gratitude and our capacity to recognize that for which we might be grateful. The more we express our thanks, the more things we can see for which to be thankful. It's as if whatever the gravity of what currently requires our focus, we are always developing a peripheral vision of gratitude that is increasingly aware of far more than we can actually attend to. We acquire a competence to see that which will color and inform our focus in helpful, healthful ways.

Suggesting Hope

Bodies crowded around. Coffee painting the morning air. Me alone in the crowd, cherishing a gift I have not begun to appreciate. My heart rises in standing ovation for this otherness that defies categorizing. Not sweetness per se. Distinct like a good strong coffee. Unique, yet still me—dawn surprising us with the consistent repetition of a completely new day.

The sun warms the chilled morning air and suggests hope from a quarter about which I did not know. In a form I could not recognize. Overlooked possibility available at one's fingertips.

Negative Space

Moving. Moving. Keeping the pace just frenetic enough to block out conflicting data. Every once in a while, though, an unexpected pause shows up, and, in the negative space, an image takes form. An insight, a perspective, a nuance. The beauty that we normally would have rushed past; the quiet voice typically drowned out by all the noise; the nourishing tidbit that we do not savor because we scarf so much junk.

Since the gift comes from elsewhere, we cannot control it or request it on demand. We can only create space or crowd out the space for it to appear when it will. Moving. Pausing. Moving.

The Realm of Forgiveness

Living out of forgiveness is dangerous. To partake in a redemptive story so much bigger than myself is to wander lost even while the story line asserts I'm found. To be significant in the story without being central is easier to preach than navigate.

There are no markers. The roads aren't paved. The traveling companions are few, and the guides are non-existent.

Forgiveness speaks of an orientation toward life, hope and the pervasive devastation of sin, by which the reality of sin does not dominate the story of life (i.e. make the story line one of overcoming sin), but is yet another venue for the redemptive power of God to manifest itself on behalf of those he loves.

How can I be so fully, perfectly, and unconditionally loved and not have the focus of the story shift onto me and the adequacy of my response to this love? And how can the story of my response to this love fail to turn on the never-resolved problem of my sinfulness?

Hence the disorienting mystery of forgiveness and the meta-story of redemption. The very framework of how I perceive reality itself has failed me and all I serve. And while I feel my way along the outskirts of this realm, all is a blur of swirling and undulating impressions. Maps and roads and markers are not the tools of navigation in this world. I am beginning to sense that forgiveness and prayer are key, and that the overarching schema is a redemptive one.

Forgiven. I am just beginning to comprehend its implications.

Peace from Elsewhere

For some life seems so ordered, stable and grounded. Some variation of the opposite for the rest of us. I have to wonder to what extent that ordered community is the exception or the rule. I suspect the former. That inner turbulence is normative and outer turbulence is difficult to avoid, is the western soul/life. Hence the need for help; for assistance from outside this system; for rescue by one better and stronger and who cares enough to act.

Heads Up

The steam rising from my mug dispassionately promises to scald my over-eager tongue. The precautionary sip is too small to either sting or satisfy. Inhaling deeply I warm my shivering fingers with a two-fisted grip so that at least two of my senses are sated while I mull the approaching day.

The hills lounge comfortably outside my window gossiping idly among themselves. Their undulating contours shelter as many as they swallow, while the furtive souls at their feet scurry, heads down, anywhere but here. The bright sun teases with clarity even as it blinds.

It is my turn to step out into the coursing stream of activity that will be my day. I will keep my head up.

Fitting In

Damn conventional wisdom. I'm tired of the sugary sweet rhetorical questions laced with spirit quenching fear. All the socially sanctioned definitions of success or responsibility or life that have nothing to do with anything except stroking someone else's ego. I need to go with my own intuition. Trust my gut. I haven't got to this point in life to instructed like a school boy. (Unless, that is, I conduct myself like a school boy.)

No. We are going forward. Any and all are welcome to come along. Those more comfortable watching from the sidelines are free to do so. I won't be in the vicinity to hear your perfect hindsight.

Spreading Smile

Sketching backdrops of hope with a borrowed pencil. New worlds emerge in the negative space, where searching hearts seldom linger. Gratitude's selective memory compels out of rumored credibility alone. Poise assumed with no assurance of vindication. My spreading smile puzzles even me.

Creating the Day

While the rain scrubs the sky outside, classical music fills the air where I cradle my coffee and create the new day into which I will step. My lungs swell and I find myself owning the room, filling the awkward gaps hewn by fear.

Gift received, gift offered. Glistening eye contact celebrating an unexpected friend, and the universe responds to my resolve and poise. What sort of day shall we create?

Poise and Tension

Poised for more than I can currently handle. Mounting tensions begging to be resolved. The future, though, cannot unfold trying to resolve what is by nature complex. In fact, the capacity to hold conflicting dynamics in tension, however painful, emerges as the training from which my poise can mature. I become a listener before a reactor. One who acts out of the poise of the balanced martial artist, both cautious observer and aggressive participant. Poise finds its strength in the midst of tension and dissipates in its absence. I come alive and live most fully in the midst of life's complexities, not in the resolution of them.

This is My Prayer

I reach out beyond the scarred edges of my
  own periphery
Fragments of a soul assaulted by unseen powers
Touching down occasionally
But always in uncharted territory, unfamiliar
  terrain.

Morning prayers stain my cheeks
Gratitude and fear tug along overlapping
  trajectories
But it's all foreplay and no consummation
The sirens of wholeness are up to no good.

I reach out in hope that someone will engage
Draw me into life, protect me from
  disintegration
Train me in readiness, embolden me to step
  forward
Break out in a wide smile when I show up each
  day

Anoint and bless, sustain and vindicate
Enthusiastically commit to my well-being.

There you have it.

Made in the USA
San Bernardino, CA
10 November 2018